W. [handwritten, illegible] Man[...]
Chicago AAR - Palm Home
11-10-1973

P9-ECM-263

CHRISTOLOGY AND A MODERN PILGRIMAGE

A DISCUSSION WITH NORMAN PERRIN

edited by

Hans Dieter Betz

Published by

Society of Biblical Literature

1971

Copyright © 1971, by the SOCIETY OF BIBLICAL LITERATURE

Published 1971

Second Printing 1973

ISBN 0-88414-000-8

LETTER OF CONGRATULATIONS

Dear Norman:

The members of the New Testament Colloquium have asked me to present these pages, together with our congratulations, to you at your 50th birthday on November 30.

Your paper entitled "Towards an Interpretation of the Gospel of Mark" was discussed at this year's meeting on October 23 in the home of Hans Jonas. Edward Hobbs presented his critique during that meeting, too. In addition to this discussion Eldon Epp, Victor Furnish, Helmut Koester, James Robinson, and Amos Wilder have written essays dealing with your major publications.

We hope that you will favorably accept these papers. They are more than a testimony of personal sympathy and friendship. Knowing you we are aware that you want us to take your concerns and your scholarship seriously. This summer when I sent letters out asking people to make contributions their response was immediate and enthusiastic. As usual there was a little more enthusiasm than realism, so that not all were able to complete their papers on time.

However, if such an unusual enterprise succeeds in spite of all obstacles, it is due to the stimulation you have given to the Colloquium. The way in which it succeeds is not all that unfamiliar to those who know Norman Perrin.

Hans Dieter Betz

Claremont, California
November 27, 1970

TABULA GRATULATORIAE

Professor J. C. Beker
Princeton Theological Seminary

Professor Hans Dieter Betz
School of Theology at Claremont

Professor Raymond E. Brown
Union Theological Seminary

Professor Eldon J. Epp
Case Western Reserve University

Professor Joseph A. Fitzmyer
Fordham University

Professor Robert W. Funk
University of Montana

Professor Victor P. Furnish
Southern Methodist University

Professor Dieter Georgi
Harvard Divinity School

Professor Paul Hammer
Colgate Rochester Divinity School

Professor Edward C. Hobbs
Graduate Theological Union

Professor Hans Jonas
New School of Social Research

Professor Helmut Koester
Harvard Divinity School

Professor Robert A. Kraft
University of Pennsylvania

Professor George MacRae
Weston College

Professor Paul W. Meyer
Vanderbilt University

Professor James M. Robinson
Claremont Graduate School

Professor John Strugnell
Harvard Divinity School

Professor Amos N. Wilder
Harvard Divinity School

Professor Wilhelm Wuellner
Pacific School of Religion

TABLE OF CONTENTS

Towards an Interpretation of the Gospel of Mark

by Norman Perrin

A member of the "Chicago School" of literary critics, R. S. Crane, challenges us to begin a consideration of a given text by asking the question of what was, for the author, "the primary intuition of form which enabled him to synthesize his materials into an ordered whole," by seeking the "shaping principle" which led the author to cast his work in the particular form in which he did cast it, and not in another.[1] So far as the texts of the New Testament are concerned this challenge is perhaps particularly appropriate in the case of the gospel of Mark and the two volume gospel of Luke and Acts of the Apostles. It is true that neither Mark nor Luke[2] are subtly concerned with such matters as plot structure and character development in the manner of a Shakespeare or a Henry Fielding, two authors Crane discusses in this context, but they are authors and there is a sense in which they must consciously have shaped their work: they both create new wholes out of existing smaller units of tradition. There is no structured narrative gospel before Mark and no Acts of the Apostles before Luke. It is appropriate therefore to begin an interpretation of the gospel of Mark or of Luke-Acts with a structural analysis of the works and to seek the purpose of the authors in those structures.

Our concern is to interpret the gospel of Mark and so we will begin by offering a structural analysis of that gospel as a whole and then of the central section, 8:22-10:52, in more detail since this section is generally recognized as that in which Mark particularly interprets his own work.

Then we will turn to those matters in the gospel which are clearly
very important to an understanding of the text as a whole: the predictions of the passion and resurrection, the relationship between the passion and the parousia of Jesus in the gospel, and the so-called "messianic secret." In the course of this discussion we shall avail ourselves
of the insights gained from the structural analysis as well as the more
conventional methods of the New Testament scholarship, and we will also
deliberately avail ourselves of insights to be derived from a general
(i.e., non-biblical) literary critical consideration of the gospel of
Mark. A true interpretation of the gospel must be built upon that
which is peculiar to it as a discrete text, in this instance particularly the structure, upon that which it shares with its related texts, in
this instance the remaining texts of the New Testament, and upon that
which it has in common with other literary texts, in this instance such
general literary critical considerations as the movement of the plot,
the roles of the protagonists, and the like. So the methodology to be
pursued in this paper will be a combination of structural analysis,
biblical criticism, and general literary criticism. At the conclusion
of the paper we will take up the general question of the purpose of
Mark in light of our previous discussion and at that time we will look
briefly at the structure and purpose of Mark in perspective.

I.   The Structure of the Gospel of Mark

There has been considerable discussion of the structure of Mark
and there are therefore some points at which we can simply draw on generally accepted opinion.   It would be generally recognized that there
is a broad, although by no means precise, geographical outline to the
gospel. We may take that given by V. Taylor[3] as representative:

1:1-13	Introduction
1:14-6:13	Galilee
6:14-8:26	Beyond Galilee
8:27-10:52	Caesarea Philippi to Jerusalem
11:1-16:8	Jerusalem

It is valid to recognize the significance of geographical data for Mark
because he himself attaches real significance to it, as we shall have
occasion to note further below.

Another characteristic of Mark as an author is that he composes
Sammelberichte and inserts them into his narratives, as has been recognized since K. L. Schmidt's seminal Die Rahmen der Geschichte Jesu.[4]
These Sammelberichte are: 1:14-15, 21-22, 39; 2:13; 3:7-12; 5:21; 6:6b,
12-13, 30-33, 53-56; 10:1. It would be natural for such summaries to
come at divisions in the narrative, marking the transition from one section to another,[5] and so where we find them in conjunction with a change
in geographical locale we may assume that here we do have such divisions.
This would give us the following structure:

1:1-13	Introduction
1:14-15	Transitional Markan summary

1:16-3:6	Galilee
3:7-12	Transitional Markan summary
3:13-6:6a	
6:6b	Transitional Markan summary
6:7-8:26	Beyond Galilee
8:27-10:52	Caesarea Philippi to Jerusalem
11:1-16:8	Jerusalem

We can take our analysis a stage further by noting that there are only two giving of sight stories in the gospel and that they are to be found at the beginning and end of the geographical section, Caesarea Philippi to Jerusalem, and that each one of them does in fact have a geographical reference of its own: 8:22-26 Bethsaida; 10:46-52 Jericho. We may therefore regard these as serving as transitional units and accept the division:

8:22-26	Transitional giving of sight story
8:27-10:45	
10:46-52	Transitional giving of sight story.

Within the section 11:1-16:8 the aids to recognizing divisions we have used so far fail us but then their place is taken by the fact that in this section we have obvious sense units. The passion narrative proper clearly begins at 14:1; and chapter 13 stands out as being devoted entirely to the only extended speech of Jesus in the gospel apart from the parabolic discourse of chapter 4. So we have the division:

11:1-12:44	Jerusalem
13:1-37	Apocalyptic discourse
14:1-16:8	Passion narrative

The last point to be noted is that both the apocalyptic discourse and the passion narrative have an introduction: 13:1-5a sets the stage for 5b-37, and the plot between the authorities and Judas 14:1-2, 10-12, sets the stage for the passion narrative.[6]

All in all this gives us the following basic analysis of the gospel of Mark,

STRUCTURAL ANALYSIS OF THE GOSPEL OF MARK

1:1-13	Introduction
1:14-15	Transitional Markan summary
1:16-3:6	First major section
3:7-12	Transitional Markan summary
3:13-6:6a	Second major section
6:6b	Transitional Markan summary
6:7-8:22	Third major section
8:23-26	Transitional giving of sight story
8:27-10:45	Fourth major section
10:46-52	Transitional giving of sight story
11:1-12:44	Fifth major section
13:1-5a	Introduction to the apocalyptic discourse
13:5b-37	Apocalyptic discourse
14:1-2, 10-12	Introduction to the passion narrative with intercalation 3-9
14:13-16:8	Passion narrative

There are a number of points about this analysis which will concern us in detail later. In the first place it should be noted that one of the strongest arguments for the validity of the analysis and an

important point for the interpretation of the gospel is that every major
section ends on a note which looks forward to the passion:

3:6	the plot to destroy Jesus
6:6a	Jesus' rejection by "his own"
8:22	the misunderstanding of the disciples
10:45	the ransom saying

Then, after the second transitional giving of sight story with its
location in Jericho, there is no further transitional unit but rather
a kind of double barreled climax to the gospel as a whole: the apocalyptic discourse and the passion narrative, each with its own introduction.
The significance of these points will concern us later.

II. The Structure of Mark 8:22-10:52

There is general agreement that in this section of the gospel Mark sets out his own understanding and interpretation of the passion of Jesus and of its significance for Christian discipleship in his own church and among his own readers. Since the Markan purpose is very close to the surface in this section it will be worth our while to analyse it in detail.

We may begin again by noting the geographical data which this time consists not of a broad geographical outline but of quite specific references, as follows:

8:22	Bethsaida
8:27	Caesarea Philippi
9:30	Galilee (9:33 Capernaum)
10:1	Judea and beyond Jordan
10:32	On the way to Jerusalem
10:46	Jericho

Each of these geographical references introduces a new section. The first and last, the transitional giving of sight stories, we need not discuss further but the remaining four need to be discussed in some detail.

The first and most obvious thing about the geographical references is that three of them introduce predictions of the passion and resurrection (henceforth simply: predictions): 8:27; 9:30; 10:32. Indeed we can go even further than that, for the sections including the predictions are units of markedly parallel construction:

Prediction	8:31	9:31	10:33-34

| Misunderstanding | 8:32-33 | 9:32 | 10:35-41 |
| Teaching about discipleship | 8:34-9:1 | 9:33-37 | 10:42-45 |

So a first basic division we may make is the following:

8:27	Caesarea Philippi
8:27-30	Peter's confession
8:31-9:1	First prediction unit
9:30	Galilee (9:33 Capernaum)
9:30-37	Second prediction unit
10:1	Judea and beyond Jordan
10:32	On the way to Jerusalem
10:33-45	Third prediction unit

We can move a stage further by noting a further feature of the Markan compositional technique, the use of time references.

Mark uses time references to link together originally separate units of tradition so as to give them an integral connection. So in 2:1 "... he returned to Capernaum after some days.." links together the collection of acts of power in Capernaum and Galilee, 1:21-45, with the collection of controversy stories which reaches its climax in 3:6, so giving us the major division 1:14-3:6. Again, 4:35, "on that day," links the parable chapter with the crossing of the sea and the tradition which follows it. Interesting are 11:12, "on the following day," and 11:20, "as he passed by in the morning," which are Markan redactional references whereby he is able to separate the fig tree story into two parts and yet hold it together while intercalating the cleansing of the temple.

In the unit between 8:27 and 9:30 there is just such a time reference: 9:2, "And after six days... ." In accordance with what we have
noted about Mark's use of these references it must be held to indicate
a further division between 8:27-9:1 and 9:2-30, and to be a redactional
link which stresses an integral relationship between the Caesarea
Philippi passion prediction unit and the Transfiguration. The fact
that it functions in this way and that it parallels in this respect
other time references in Mark means that we must take it as Markan redaction and not as residual tradition. The "after six days" rather
than some other interval is of real significance for Mark, as is the
intentional link between Caesarea Philippi and the Mount of Transfiguration. We shall return to these points later.

The account of the Transfiguration, 9:2-9, is carefully linked to
the following discussion about Elijah the forerunner, 9:11-13, by a
redactional command to secrecy, 9:9-10, but that leaves us with a kind
of appendix: 9:14-29, the boy with the dumb spirit. At this point we
recall that among the elements in this whole section not yet accounted
for is that between the second prediction unit and the geographical
reference to Judea (10:1), 9:38-50, the non-disciple who practised exor-
cisms in the name of Jesus. These two pericopes share a good deal in
common. In the first place they are each appended to major units within the narrative, the first to the transfiguration-Elijah unit, and the
second to the second prediction unit. Then, secondly, they are curi-
ously related in that the first concerns disciples unsuccessful in
exorcism and the second a non-disciple successful in exorcism. Then,
thirdly, they both have the characteristic structure of incident

followed by teaching to the disciples. It seems reasonable therefore
to treat them as symmetrical appendices to successive ajor units in
the narrative as a whole. Seen in this way they also function well in
the movement of the section as a whole. After the first prediction
unit and the closely related transfiguration unit we get the only exorcism practised by Jesus in the gospel of Mark after 8:22, and the account emphasizes the contrast between the faith of the boy's father,
demanded by Jesus, and the inability of the disciples. After the second prediction unit we get a successful exorcist in the name of Jesus
who is not an actual disciple. Mark is throwing the failure of the
disciples themselves into very sharp relief. Then he has appended the
teaching of 9:41-50 at that point as appropriate to the theme of the
section.

The only part of the whole section now unaccounted for is that
beginning with the reference to Judea, 10:1-31. This consists of three
parallel units each having the structure of incident-teaching to disciples. They are therefore appropriately placed in a section of the
gospel in which discipleship is a major theme and structurally they may
be regarded as intercalated between the second and third prediction
units.

We arrive then at the following detailed analysis of Mark 8:22-
10:52.

STRUCTURAL ANALYSIS OF MARK 8:22-10:52

I.   8:22-26   Bethsaida transitional giving of sight story

II.   8:27   Caesarea Philippi

     A. 8:27-30   Fundamental narrative of Peter's confession

     B. 8:31-9:1 First prediction unit

       1. Prediction 8:31
       2. Misunderstanding 8:32-33
       3. Teaching about discipleship 8:34-9:1

III.   9:2   "After six days..."

     A. 9:2-8   Transfiguration

     B. 9:9-13   Elijah as forerunner

     C. 9:14-29   Appended incident and teaching on discipleship

       1. Disciples and boy with the dumb spirit 9:14-27
       2. Teaching to disciples 9:28-29

IV.   9:30   Galilee   (9:33 Capernaum)

     A. 9:30-37   Second prediction unit

       1. Prediction 9:31
       2. Misunderstanding 9:32
       3. Teaching about discipleship 9:33-37

     B. 9:38-50   Appended incident and teaching on discipleship

       1. Non disciple practising exorcism 9:38-40
       2. Teaching to disciples 9:41-50

V.   10:1   Judea and beyond Jordan   Intercalated units of incident and teaching to disciples

     A. 10:2-12   Divorce

       1. The Pharisees and divorce 10:1-9
       2. Teaching to disciples   10:10-12

Before leaving the structural analysis of 8:22-10:52 we should perhaps call attention to the function of the account of Peter's confession within the whole section. Clearly it serves a major purpose. It is the point of departure for the first prediction unit and is presupposed by each of the following prediction units. But beyond that it is the pivotal point of the whole section. Every unit in the section, except the transfiguration unit which serves to interpret the predictions, as we shall see, is concerned with discipleship in one way or another and each one therefore pivots on Peter's confession. A consequence of this is that the confession is essentially separate from the first prediction unit and independent of it. Matthew testifies to this when he separates the two and inserts between them the account of the revelation to and commissioning of Peter, which probably originated in a narrative of a resurrection appearance to Peter. Together with the carefully structured parallelism of the prediction units this indepen-

dence suggests that the original pre-Markan tradition was of a Petrine
confession and that the addition of the prediction unit is by Mark
himself.[7]

III.   The Predictions of the Passion and Resurrection
                     Mark 8:31; 9:31; 10:32-33

Like so much else in connection with the study of Mark the discussion of the predictions virtually begins with William Wrede who in
1901 argued that in them we have before us "the naked expression of
conceptions of the early Christian community and nothing more."[8]   It
took some fifty years for this opinion to become generally accepted;
as late as 1952 a commentator as important as V. Taylor could blandly
ignore it![9]   But it now is generally accepted; the most that could be
urged today is that some small part of one of them may go back to an
original saying of Jesus, and that simply amounts to saying that constituent parts of the predictions are pre-Markan, which is certainly
true.[10]

With the general acceptance of the position of Wrede we are in a
position to appreciate the contributions made to the discussion of the
predictions by scholars who stood in the tradition established by him,
and in this connection two that are particularly important are M. Dibelius and E. Lohmeyer.

Dibelius argued that the predictions were "introduced by the col-
lecting evangelist" into traditional material now to be found in Mark
8-10 "to show how and why the passion and death was willed by God."[11]
The predictions themselves were "the preaching of the (Markan) church
about the Son of Man"[12] and what Mark has done is to take these sayings
from his church and introduce them into the traditional material he has
in chapters 8-10 of his gospel so as to interpret the passion in its
divine necessity.   In his discussion of the use to which the evangelist

has put the predictions Dibelius has been echoed by every subsequent
commentator and correctly so, but that the predictions themselves existed as complete sayings in the pre-Markan tradition, or in the Markan
church, came more from Dibelius' view of the evangelists themselves
than from any discussion of the evidence in the matter. Both Dibelius
and Bultmann had a low estimate of the evangelists as authors, thinking
of them as collectors and editors of tradition who were by no means
masters of their material. This was probably justifiable in terms of
the form critical work of the 1920s but the problem is that it has
tended to live on in more recent German work and to inhibit therefore
the discussion of the role of Mark himself in the literary formation of
the predictions. This is a point to which we shall return below.

After Dibelius the only scholarly discussion of the predictions
which matters from our perspective is that by E. Lohmeyer in his Meyer
commentary, originally published in 1937. Lohmeyer's commentary is in
many respects a classic, especially in its concern for the method and
meaning of the evangelist's compositional activity. So in the matter
of the predictions he argued that there was an original saying like
that now found in Luke 17:25--without going into the question of its
authenticity--and that the predictions now in Mark have been developed
from it. He then shows how this threefold development is meaningful
in terms of Mark's didactic purpose and the thrust of the Markan narrative. The first prediction subordinates everything to the dei and so
stresses the necessity for the passion, the second varies between the
present and future tenses and so stresses the actuality of that which
must take place, and the third is entirely in the future tense and so

emphasizes the movement towards the events which are now depicted in detail.[13]

With the rise of redaction criticism the focus of attention changed and now came to be concentrated on the specific redactional and compositional activity of Mark in the predictions as well as upon the function of the predictions in the gospel as a whole. The first redaction critic to take up the predictions was H. E. Tödt who discussed them in the course of his epoch making investigation of the Son of Man in the synoptic tradition.[14] He made a number of valuable points, especially about the "train of terms" used in the predictions, but he was too much under the influence of the Dibelius-Bultmann view of the evangelist to consider anything more than formation in the tradition. Mark inherits each one as a unit, even the third "was not formed by Mark either," because the details do not correspond to those of the passion narrative in Mark.[15]

F. Hahn took up the predictions in his investigation of the history of the use of christological titles in earliest Christianity, specifically in pre-Markan tradition.[16] He too was of the opinion that the real formulation of the predictions in his narrative and in comparatively minor redaction of them. So he finds two basic types of Son of Man sayings concerning the passion, one not referring to scripture (Mark 10:33f; 14:41b; 9:31) and one referring to scripture (Mark 14:21; 8:31). So the first and second predictions (8:31; 9:31) are to be distinguished from one another as representing the two originally distinct types of saying, while the third (10:33f.) has been produced by the evangelist Mark by redaction of the second. Hahn rightly rejects Tödt's contention that the differences between the saying and the passion narrative itself in Mark ruled out this possibility.

The advances over Tödt here are (1) that it is recognized that 10:33f. is a Markan literary production, and (2) that the real differences between the first prediction on the one hand and the second and third on the other are recognized. But this second point only throws into sharper relief the fact that the last part of all three predictions is almost verbally identical. This verbal identity cries out for explanation and certainly rules out the possibility that we have here two originally quite distinct types of saying; the more so since the uniform "after three days" of the resurrection is to all intents and purposes without parallel in this context in the New Testament, even in dependent passages!

The third redaction critic to take up the predictions was G. Strecker who wrote an essay on them which has been published in both German and English.[17] Still unable to shake the Dibelius-Bultmann view of the evangelist Mark to the extent of considering Markan literary activity in all three predictions, he none the less advanced over Tödt and Hahn to the point of recognizing that both the second and third predictions are Markan literary productions, arguing that they have been produced by redaction of the first, and he recognized also that he had to argue that the first was pre-Markan. His arguments for this are as follows: (1) The "after three days" contradicts the passion narrative, Mark 14:58; 15:29, and the use of anistanai is non-Markan, Mark normally prefers egeirein. (2) Mark normally prefers stauroun to apokteinein. (3) The reference to "elders, chief priests and scribes," i.e. the full

Sanhedrin, is non-Markan since Mark abbreviates it elsewhere in the predictions. Then (4) the reference to Psalm 118:22 in apodokimasthenai and (5) the use of dei are traditional rather than Markan.

These arguments are of very different weight. (1) in effect calls attention to the last element in the predictions which does require explanation. But there is no reason a priori why this explanation should be Markan use of tradition rather than real significance for the Markan theology and purpose.[18] (2) breaks down on the observation that in the synoptics the verb stauroun is found only in the passion narrative, and the fact that the use of apokteinein is susceptible of a different explanation, as we shall see below. (3) tends to show the exact opposite i.e. Markan composition, because the same phrase is found in Mark 14:53 where a strong element of Markan redactional activity is generally recognized. (4) and (5) do no more than show that the prediction contains traditional elements. All in all it may be said that Strecker successfully argues for pre-Markan elements in 8:31, and that he calls attention to the "after three days" and the use of anistanai as requiring explanation, but that he falls far short of proving the existence of Mark 8:31 as a unit before Mark.

The discussion of the predictions by Tödt, Hahn and Strecker has not therefore resolved the problem of the origin of the predictions themselves but it did have the result of showing that they have not been developed from a saying like that now found in Luke 17:25 (The Son of Man must suffer many things and be rejected [apodokimastenai]) or Mark 9:12b (The Son of Man should suffer many things and be treated with contempt [exoudēnethē]). Strecker showed that the former has been

created by Luke by redaction from the prediction in Mark 8:31[19] and
Tödt saw that the latter is "an independent statement which issued from
the debates of the Christians with the Jews... ."[20] We will take up
that last point below.

We have reached a stage in our discussion of the interpretation of
Mark similar to the one we have reached in Life of Jesus research, the
point namely where the question of the burden of proof becomes all important. Other things being equal, is a saying in Mark to be regarded
as tradition, redaction or Markan composition? Put in that way of
course the question is simply unanswerable but it does make the point
that all three things are possible and one should not automatically assume one rather than another. Standing in the shadow of Dibelius and
Bultmann the tendency is to assume tradition unless the opposite can be
proven, and in reaction against that the tendency might become to see
Markan composition unless the opposite can be proven. But an investigation of the text of Mark reveals all three types of sayings present
side by side. In a study of the Caesarea Philippi pericope itself I
argued that the teaching in 8:34-37 consists of originally independent
sayings editorially associated by Mark, in which process he had predecessors, or in the terms we are now using: tradition. 8:38, on the
other hand has been produced by Markan redaction of a _Satz_ _heiligen_
Rechtes which originally had two parts, in which opinion I was following Käsemann. 9:1 however I argued was a Markan composition modelled
on an apocalyptic promise like that now found in Mark 13:30.[21] Whatever may be the merits of those particular arguments the time has come
to recognize that Mark does indeed editorially use and arrange tradi-

tional material, redact existing material in various ways, and create
wholly new material, not excluding sayings that he puts on the lips of
Jesus. This being the case the necessity is to examine each instance
on its merits and not to make assumptions too readily.

In the case of the predictions there are a number of things to
be said. In the first place the analysis of 8:22-10:52 shows how carefully structured the three prediction units are, and how basic they are
to the structure of the section as a whole. Then, secondly, they fit
their present context and function so smoothly that it is hard to con-
ceive of them as ever having had any other _Sitz_; as it is equally hard
to think of the present _Sitz_ as anything other than Markan.[22] Then,
thirdly and conversely, the sheer extent of the Markan literary activity in the Caesarea Philippi pericope as a whole and in the teaching
of 8:34-9:1 suggest the probability that he has been similarly active
in 8:31.

These considerations are such as to suggest that when we consider
the predictions we may not assume that they are traditional unless the
opposite can be proven. If any assumption is justified it is rather
that Mark has composed them, most probably using traditional material
but using it creatively.

In discussing synoptic gospel texts it is best to approach them
systematically by considering in turn the three possible _Sitze_ which
form and redaction criticism has taught us to recognize: the _Sitz im
Evangelium_, the _Sitz im Leben der Kirche_, the _Sitz im Leben Jesu_. We
now turn to such a discussion of the predictions of the passion and
resurrection in the gospel of Mark.

In the question of the _Sitz im Evangelium_ we are on firm, not to say well travelled ground, for whatever may be the case about their literary composition there is no doubt but that Dibelius was right about their purpose being to show "how and why the passion was willed by God," and this is the universal opinion of commentators both before and after Dibelius. Our structural analysis bears this out, for obviously the prediction units are fundamental to the structure of 8:22-10:52 and hence to the movement of the "plot" of the gospel as a whole. But there is something more to be said because our analysis revealed also how impregnated with the discipleship theme the whole section of the gospel is that is so carefully set between the symbolically significant giving of sight stories. Moreover the prediction units themselves hinge on Peter's confession and each and every one climaxes in teaching about discipleship. So we can say that the purpose of the predictions is not only to interpret the passion but to interpret discipleship in light of the passion, and that here as elsewhere Mark is quite clearly and deliberately addressing his own readers through the mouth of Jesus.

There is a third thing that can be said about the Markan purpose in the predictions and that is that they are part of the totality of the literary devices by means of which Mark sets out to correct the false christology of his own day. I have argued this in some detail elsewhere[23] and I need do no more here than point to the way in which Mark sets up the title "Christ" in Peter's confession and then immediately interprets that by using "Son of Man" in the prediction. In 14:61f., where there is strong Markan redaction, we find "Son of God"

also immediately interpreted by a use of "Son of Man." If I may plagiarize myself Mark uses Son of Man creatively to present his own christology and in so doing he creates the threefold emphasis upon present
authority, necessary suffering and apocalyptic judgment which that title
carries in his gospel. There was a certain amount of preparation for
it in the tradition of the church, but the full development is Markan.
In this development the predictions play a major part.

There is therefore no particular problem about the predictions
and their Sitz im Evangelium. It is however different when we come to
inquire into the Sitz im Leben der alten Kirche, for here we have the
problem of how much of the predictions are traditional. In view of the
arguments given above in connection with the question of the burden of
proof, I believe I am justified in putting the question not in the form
"do the predictions have a previous Sitz in the tradition of the church?"
but in the form, "do the individual parts of the predictions have Sitze
in the pre-Markan tradition of the church?" We now turn to a discussion of the question in this form.

A.   The use of Son of Man

Perhaps the most striking feature about the predictions is the fact
that they are all in the form of Son of Man sayings. As I noted above
the reason for this is that Mark is developing a complex christology and
using Son of Man as its vehicle. The three uses of Son of Man which he
develops, authority in the present (2:10; 2:28), necessary suffering
(the predictions) and apocalyptic judgment (8:38), are his but there
was a certain amount of preparation for them in the tradition of the
church. In particular the church had developed the use of Son of Man

in Sätze heiligen Rechtes and in apocalyptic sayings such as Mark 13:26, and had used Son of Man in reflecting on the ministry of Jesus as a whole (Matt. 13:37; Luke 19:10), and in connection with the passion, (Mark 14:21, 41), texts we will discuss below. So the ground was prepared for Mark but the fact remains that his use of Son of Man was an act of literary creativity.

B. The use of _paradidonai_ in connection with the passion[24]

A basic element in the passion predictions is their use of the verb _paradidonai_, which is fundamental to both the second and the third predictions (9:31, "The Son of Man will be delivered into...," 10:32, "The Son of Man will be delivered to..."). This use of Son of Man with _paradidonai_ in connection with the passion of Jesus is a well marked tradition in the early church. It begins in a purely descriptive use, describing the passion of Jesus in accordance with a usage established in Jewish literature in connection with the fate of the prophets. In this sense we find the use of the verb in the passion narrative (Mark 15:1, 10, 15, 35c.) and in the stylized representation of Judas (Matthew 10:4 and frequently). The specifically Christian use begins in early Christian passion apologetic where it is used with Son of Man to stress the divine necessity for the passion. The clearest remnants of this tradition are Mark 14:21, "The Son of Man goes as it is written of him, but woe to that man by whom the Son of Man _paradidotai_," and 14:41, "...the Son of Man _paradidotai_ into the hands of sinners," of which the latter is certainly pre-Markan.[25] From this apologetic use there developed a soteriological use which had its origins in Palestinian Christianity but which reaches its fullest development in Hellenistic Jewish Christianity, and is now represented by Romans 4:25; Mark 10:45,[26] I Timothy 2:6; Titus 2:14; Galatians 1:4, 2:20; Ephesians 5:2, 5:25; Romans 8:32.

If this hypothesis about the use of paradidonai in connection with the passion is correct, then we have a concrete source for Mark's use of Son of Man and paradidonai in his passion predictions. For this constituent part of his passion predictions he is mining an aspect of the passion apologetic of earliest Palestinian Christianity.

C.   The reference to "suffer many things and be rejected," 8:31

It is clear that we have to take with this the "suffer many things and be treated with contempt" of Mark 9:12b and the "suffer many things and be rejected" of Luke 17:25. They are both redactional insertions into their present context. Mark 9:12b has been inserted by someone other than Mark into the text of the gospel[27] and Luke 17:25 has been inserted into the text of a collection of sayings taken originally from Q by the evangelist.[28] It is possible that Luke is dependent on Mark 9:12b if that stood in his text of Mark (he omits the Elijah passage) or that both Luke and the glossator of Mark are dependent on Mark 8:31, but the variant "be treated with contempt" (exoudenethe) for "be rejected" (apodokimasthenai) is in any case significant as revealing contact with early Christian passion apologetic.

A group of texts in the New Testament testify to the use of Psalm 118 with its "stone which the builders apedokimasen" in early Christian passion apologetic: Mark 12:10; I Peter 2:4; Acts 4:11. The last of these exhibits a word play in that it has exouthenetheis where one would expect a use of the LXX word apodokimazein. The introduction of this word here, and in Mark 9:12b, could be a reference to Isaiah 53:3

where in some Greek versions, but not LXX, we find exoudenemēnos. But it is more probably an allusion to Psalm 22 (LXX 21):7, exoudenēma, and 25, exoudenōsen, a Psalm used extensively in early Christian passion apologetic, as the passion narrative itself shows. In any case, this kind of word play is characteristic of the use of the Old Testament in early Christianity (and at Qumran) and is what one would expect therefore in early Christian passion apologetic.

The "be rejected" of Mark 8:31 and the "be treated with contempt" of Mark 9:12b are therefore both allusions to the use of Psalm 118 and Psalm 22 in Christian passion apologetic and the "be rejected" of Luke 17:25 is also such an allusion, either directly or at second hand through Mark.

What is the case with the "suffer many things"?

There is no instance of the use of this phrase in connection with the passion except in Mark and in dependence on Mark in the New Testament. The verb "to suffer" came to be used inclusively of the passion and death of Jesus in early Christianity, e.g., Luke 24:26, but the use here of the events of the passion apart from the death itself is without parallel, and it is of course in keeping with the recital of the events themselves in the third prediction. It is possible therefore that here we are dealing with a Markan construction. This possibility would be strengthened if we could construe the polla as an adverb, for such an adverbial use is characteristically Markan, but it may be here the object of the verb as it is in Mark 5:26, which is traditional rather than redactional.

D.   The reference to "killing" and to "rising after three days"

The final part of the passion predictions, the reference to the
death and resurrection, are the most stereotyped part of the whole.
Elsewhere there are variations between the predictions, but always we
have apokteinein, meta treis hēmeras, anistanai.   This creates the impression that here we may be dealing with a pre-formed unit, the more
so since "after three days" actually conflicts with the time span presupposed by the Markan passion narrative itself (Mark 14:58; 15:29).
But we have no evidence for the existence of such a pre-formed unit
apart from the stereotyped nature of this aspect of the predictions
themselves.   Rather we have here the same mixture of constituent parts
from earlier tradition, especially from passion apologetic, and Markan
formulation that we have observed in connection with the other parts of
the predictions, and the consistency exhibited is due to the importance
of the phrases to the Markan purpose.[29]

apokteinein is regularly used in early Christian passion apologetic with "the Jews" or its equivalent as subject.   The object is ultimately Jesus but there is a strong emphasis upon the previous fate
of "the prophets," and of the link between the fate of Jesus and that
of the prophets: Romans 11:3; I Thessalonians 2:15; Acts 3:15, 7:52.
So the use of the general "to kill" rather than the specific "to cru-
cify" in the passion predictions is due to a link with this strand of
early Christian passion apologetic.

anistanai is a verb used traditionally in connection with the resurrection, e.g., I Thessalonians 4:14, 16.   It is found, together with
"on the third day," in Hosea 6:2 ("On the third day he will raise us

up"), and this is presumably the origin of the use of the verb in early Christianity. As compared with egeirein, the other verb used in connection with the resurrection in the New Testament, anistanai is distinctive in that it can be used both transitively, in which case it is a synonym for egeirein as in Acts 2:24, and intransitively, in which case it is distinctive in that it puts the emphasis upon the rising rather than upon being raised. Jesus now raises himself and is no longer the passive object of God's handling: I Thessalonians 4:14, "Jesus died and rose again." This will have been the reason for Mark's choice of the verb in preference to egeirein; it is the appropriate verb to use with Son of Man to blend together emphases upon both suffering and power in the passion predictions. Matthew and Luke have no such theological concern and they do not maintain the verb, but Mark does have this concern and so uses anistanai uniformly in the predictions.

The use of meta treis hēmeras is extraordinarily interesting in that Mark maintains it uniformly in the predictions and Matthew and Luke as uniformly substitute "on the third day," which is both the regularly used expression in early Christian tradition, I Corinthians 15:4, and the one found in the ultimate source, Hosea 6:2. It therefore has to be assumed that "after three days" is distinctively Markan and the question has to be raised as to what significance it has for Mark.

It is often noted that the "after six days" in Mark 9:2, which I argued above redactionally links the first prediction unit with the transfiguration unit, is the only such definite time reference in Mark

outside the passion narrative. But that is to restrict oneself to
narrative and to overlook the fact that "after six days" contrasts with
the "after three days" of the predictions. I shall argue below that
the transfiguration is for Mark proleptic of the parousia of Jesus and
I therefore suggest that the contrast is deliberate: after three days,
the resurrection; after six days, the parousia. In this aspect of the
predictions therefore Mark is making a point that is very important
to him: his readers are to follow him, so to speak, through the resurrection to the parousia. We shall find ample evidence for the fact
that this is Mark's purpose below.

The predictions as a group

If our argument so far is sound then the predictions are Markan
literary productions, the individual parts being mined from early Christian tradition, especially the church's passion apologetic, but the predictions as a whole being Markan. But in this case why are there three
of them and why do they fall into two types, one using dei "suffer
many things and be rejected," and the other using paradidonai? We will
take the second question first and discuss the two different types.

First of all, the variations although real must not be exaggerated.
The use of dei certainly implies the fulfillment of scripture but then
so does the use of paradidonai with its echoes of the apologetic paradidonai tradition. Then the references to the death and the resurrection "after three days" are constant: what we have to account for is
the variation from "suffer many things and be rejected" to "be delivered to/into the hands." Here the explanation can only be that Mark has
chosen at one place to make the reference to divine necessity, physical

suffering and rejection explicit, and so takes his material from passion apologetic, and in another place links forward to the passion narrative, and so turns to the use of paradidonai. The actual order makes
sense in terms of the structure of the gospel as a whole: the rejection theme is a feature of the gospel before the predictions and the
use of paradidonai looks foward to Gethsemane and the passion narrative. There is also a kind of arresting brutality about "suffer many
things and be rejected" which accords well with its setting in the narrative structure as response to the confession of Peter.

Why is there not a third variation? Why two uses of paradidonai
rather than a third element from passion apologetic or the passion narrative? This we cannot know. Perhaps it is the influence of paradidonai in Gethsemane and the passion narrative, perhaps the lack of a
third obviously relevant traditional element: Put the other way--why
are there three predictions and not two?--the question is easier to
answer. In the first place Mark has a tendency towards threes, as Lohmeyer recognized[30] and then our structural analysis of 8:27-10:45
showed how important the three passion prediction units were to the
skeleton of the whole. With three the evangelist had room for his various appendices and intercalations; with two the structure would have
become very clumsy. Then on the positive side, the three predictions
give Mark an opportunity to express himself with some subtlety.

The first subordinates everything to the dei; the second varies
between the future and the present, and so stresses the actuality of
that which must take place; the third is entirely in the future tense
and emphasizes the movement towards the events, the picture of which

is now painted in detail.[31]   Then the three sets of teaching about discipleship also allows for considerable development and the three sets
do in fact show internal relationship and development.   For example, in
the first one, the disciple must take up the cross, as did the master;
in the second he must imitate the master in servanthood; and in the
third that servanthood is defined in a saying which combines cross and
servanthood: 10:45.

In a matter as complex as that of the predictions of the passion
and resurrection in Mark we cannot hope to have offered a convincing
solution to all the problems but we hope that we have shown that an
attention to the literary structure of the gospel and its sections can
be suggestive in discussing the role of the predictions in the gospel
and in approaching some of the questions that arise in connection with
them.   It is an element of redaction or composition criticism to which,
we would claim, more attention may be given.   One aspect of the predictions we have not yet discussed is the fact that they no where mention
the parousia, but this will come up in our next section as we discuss
the relationship between the passion and the parousia in the gospel
of Mark.

IV. The Relationship Between the Passion and the Parousia in the Gospel of Mark

Martin Kähler's dictum that the gospels are passion narratives with extended introductions has been widely held to apply particularly to Mark. Most of us who have written on the gospel have said this at one time or another; certainly I have done so myself. But the structural analysis of the gospel shows that this is true only to a limited extent. It is true to the extent that each major section of the gospel ends on a note looking forward to the passion and that the central interpretative section 8:27-10:45 is built around predictions of the passion and resurrection and climaxes in a cross saying. But the role of the cross in 8:27-10:45 is due to the importance of Jesus' sufferings for christology and discipleship, and the fact is that the climactic allusion to the cross in the woman's sacrifice is followed not by the passion narrative but by the apocalyptic discourse. Nor is it true to say that chapter 13 comes before the passion narrative and hence is subordinated to it, as does Schreiber,[32] for the analysis shows that the discourse and the passion narrative stand side by side, each with its own separate introduction, and with no transitional unit or other editorial device to subordinate the discourse to that movement of the gospel narrative towards the climax of the passion. The structural analysis shows that the gospel moves to a twin climax of apocalyptic discourse and passion narrative. Moreover, this finding by structural analysis can be supported by observation of literary relationships between the discourse and the narrative. A whole series of cross references have been noted between the two, first by R. H. Lightfoot,[33] and the cumulative effect of these is support for my contention that Mark is deliberately setting the two side by side.

But our structural analysis does more than call attention to the parallelism between the apocalyptic discourse and the passion narrative, it also calls attention to the strong link between the passion prediction units and the transfiguration unit. As Mark sees it the transfiguration unit adds something to the passion prediction units and the question is: What?

It would generally be recognized that for Mark the transfiguration of Jesus is proleptic of something,[34] either of the resurrection[35] or the parousia.[36] A case can be made out for each alternative but the weight of the evidence seems to me to indicate the parousia. (1) The Markan emphasis upon "seeing" the eschaton, 9:1, 14:62. (2) The link between 9:1 and the transfiguration itself which again indicates that we are here dealing with the eschaton. (3) The reference to Elijah and Moses best fits a parousia context. (4) The contrast between "after three days" of the predictions and "after six days" of the transfiguration indicates movement through the resurrection to the parousia, as I suggested earlier. We shall find this movement characteristic of the whole gospel. (5) 9:9, the redactional command to secrecy, indicates that Mark understands the transfiguration to be an object of interest and concern to his readers after the resurrection. This is much more likely to refer to an anticipation of the parousia than an understanding of the resurrection.[37]

If the transfiguration is for Mark proleptic of the parousia then the relationship between the passion and the parousia implied by the juxtaposition of the apocalyptic discourse and the passion narrative is supported by the link between the passion prediction units and the transfiguration unit in 8:27-10:45. But the case is even stronger than that for in the first passion prediction unit itself we move from the passion to the parousia in the teaching on discipleship, 8:34-9:1. 8:34 explicitly directs the attention of Mark's readers back to the passion ("take up his cross") and 8:34, 9:1 directs that attention forward to the imminent parousia ("when he comes...the kingdom of God come with power").

It is in this teaching in the first prediction unit that we find the clue to the actual nature of the relationship between the passion and the parousia and the function of the two things in the Markan purpose. In this teaching the risen Lord is addressing Mark's readers and the teaching itself reveals the reality of their situation: they are looking back upon the cross and forward to the parousia. In the light of the parousia they can understand the passion, for the Jesus who suffered is the one who will come as Son of Man, and in the light of parousia and the passion they can understand their own situation: they must accept the actuality of suffering in anticipation of the glory to be known at the parousia.

In view of the central role of the first prediction unit in the structure of the gospel it is not surprising that it should provide the essential clue to the situation to which the author is addressing his work. This situation comes to the fore in three other elements in the gospel and is important to an understanding of those elements: In the apocalyptic discourse itself, in 14:28 and 16:7, and in the ending of the gospel at 16:8. We will briefly consider each of these in turn.

A.   The Apocalyptic Discourse

The apocalyptic discourse has been the subject of renewed discussion since Marxsen[38] convinced us all of the importance of chapter 13 of Mark to an understanding of the situation to which the evengelist is addressing his gospel. We may not accept Marxsen's conclusions but he startled us into seeing the importance of what he was attempting. One of the important points to come up in the discussion is that of the significance of the time references which are scattered throughout the discourse and give it a redactional unity[39] which makes irrelevant the search for the original disparate sources--a search which has notably failed to achieve any agreed results but which is so much a part of our heritage that even Marxsen continues it! These references are worth listing in sequence:

Vs. 7	The end is not yet
Vs. 8	This is but the beginning of the sufferings
Vs. 10	The gospel must first be preached to all nations
Vs. 14	When you see...(let the readers understand)
Vs. 14	Then...flee to the mountains
Vs. 21	Then if any one says...do not believe it
Vs. 24	In those days, after that tribulation
Vs. 26	Then you will see...
Vs. 27	Then he will send...

The immediately obvious thing about this list is that the enigmatic "wink to the reader"[40] in verse 14 marks a definite change. Before that everything is addressed to the present of the reader, after it everything is addressed to the reader's future. As Marxsen puts it, there is here "a break in the life of the reader who is led, as it was, from present to future."[41] Conzelmann argues that there is rather more to it than that because verse 24 implies a further division; only <u>after</u> the events described in verses 14-23 does the actual parousia occur.[42] We have therefore, three groups of material in the discourse with three different time spans envisaged:

Verses 5-13	the reader's present
Verses 14-23	the reader's future, epoch 1
Verses 24-37	the reader's future, epoch 2

Moreover this division also corresponds to subtle differences in the events being described or anticipated. The first group represents realistic expectation and indeed actual experience of New Testament christians, and it has many parallels to other passages in the New Testament which deal realistically with persecution in an eschatological context, e.g., I Thess. 5:1-11; 2 Thess. 2: 1-15; Rom. 13:11-14; I Pet. 4:7; 5:8; Jas. 5:7-9.[43] The second group heightens the apocalyptic element very considerably; the expectations are still realistic but they are transposed into a much higher key. The third group abandons realistic experience altogether and the events become of a cosmic dimension; the key is now completely apocalyptic. What we have in effect is (1) actual experience of Mark's readers given an apocalyptic interpretation; (2) extrapolation from that experience to form an imminent expectation of events within the world; (3) a more distant expectation of cosmic events in which the world will be shattered and restored.

The situation to which Mark is addressing the discourse is then
that of a group of christians who are caught up in a train of events
either leading up to, or set in motion by the fall of Jerusalem and
the destruction of its temple.[44] In their situation a false eschatology
has arisen; there are false prophets and/or false messiahs[45] among them
and they have come to accept a mistaken expectation. In this situation
Mark uses the setting of the ministry of Jesus, and allows the disciples
to expose the question or express the false teaching and then puts the
correct teaching on the lips of Jesus, just as he does in the case of
the false christology he corrects by his use of Son of Man. It is for
this reason that the discourse has to come before the passion and not
after it. Chapter 13 bears many of the characteristics of a revelatory
discourse of the risen Lord to his disciples and it has recently been
argued that at one (pre-Markan) stage it did in fact have that form.[46]
Be that as it may, Mark is firmly wedded to his characteristic literary
device and the discourse precedes the passion.

I may perhaps be permitted to pause here to make the point that
the use of this literary device is the key to understanding the gospel
of Mark as a literary form. The gospel is addressed to Mark's own con-
temporaries, and Jesus addresses them directly, especially in the discipleship teaching of the prediction units and the apocalyptic discourse. Their situation and their beliefs are credited to the disciples in the narrative and so the disciples function as stage-setters,
setting the stage for the authoritative teaching of Jesus to Mark's con-
temporaries. Later the literary device was different and we have the
Risen Lord teaching his disciples the ordinances of the church in re-

velatory discourses, but for Mark the form is that of the pre-Easter
Jesus teaching his disciples. We shall go into the theological significance of this particular form later.

To return to the purpose of Mark in Chapter 13. This is more than
that of correcting a false expectation, just as Mark's purpose in the
use of Son of Man is more than that of correcting a false christology.
He intends to lead his readers firmly to the situation in which they
will gladly accept the travail and tribulation of the present and remain firm in the conviction that it will climax eventually in the coming of Jesus as Son of Man, and that they can endure what must be between now and then, as Jesus endured his passion.

B.   The role of Mark 14:28 and 16:7

In these two verses the disciples are told that after his resurrection Jesus will go before them into Galilee and there they will see
him. As in the case of the transfiguration there is a question as to
the reference intended by Mark.[47] But again the weight of the evidence
indicates that the reference is to the parousia. (1) "Seeing" in Mark
is strongly associated with the eschaton, as we argued in the case of
the transfiguration; (2) Test. Zeb. 9:8 speaks of a parousia of God in
Jerusalem in terms strikingly parallel to Mark 16:7, and the change to
Galilee is explicable in terms of the Markan purpose, as we shall argue
below; (3) in 8:27-9:1 we move from passion through resurrection to
parousia and "these supreme events do not concern the Lord only; they
are closely connected with the disciples also;"[48](4) the same sequence
is to be found in the third prediction unit where the prediction of the
passion and resurrection is followed by reference to disciple sharing

the master's "glory;" (5) 14:28 with its "after my resurrection" implies
that the event to be expected in Galilee is the third act of the drama,
death-resurrection-parousia, rather than a delayed resurrection appearance in Galilee, especially in view of the "after three days" of the
predictions and "after six days" of the transfiguration; (6) most important of all is the thrust of the whole gospel. Everywhere we find
the movement through the passion and resurrection to the parousia: in
the link between the prediction units and the transfiguration unit; in
the prediction units themselves, especially the first and the third; in
the juxtaposition of apocalyptic discourse and passion narrative, which
serves to hold in tension the passion and the parousia. It is incon-
ceivable that a climactic event explicitly and carefully referred to by
Mark[49] to take place after the passion and after the resurrection would
be a resurrection appearance and not the parousia.

The references in 14:28 and 16:7 are not therefore to a resurrection appearance in Galilee, but to the parousia. What "Galilee" indicates in this connection, we will discuss in a moment. The other sug-
gestions are that the reference is to the Gentile mission or to a secret
epiphany in Galilee. R. H. Lightfoot and his pupil C. F. Evans have
made some sound points,[50] especially about the reference to "Galilee,"
but they can be met in the context of a parousia expectation, as I
shall argue below. Schreiber's point about a secret epiphany in Galilee
is part of an altogether dubious interpretation of the gospel of Mark.[51]
But if 14:28 and 16:7 are references to the parousia, then this is very
revealing of the situation of Mark's readers. We must remember that
"the disciples and Peter" are for Mark representational figures: they

represent the christians of his own church, the readers of his gospel.
So when Jesus addresses them in 14:28 the "going before into Galilee"
is in the future because the drama of the presentation is such that the
speaker is not yet risen. But in 16:7 the tomb is empty, the Lord is
risen, and the young man addresses the readers in the present, "he is
going before you to Galilee." The situation of the readers is clearly
indicated. They are between the resurrection and the parousia, being
exhorted to follow the risen Lord to Galilee in anticipation of the
parousia.

W. Marxsen has argued this point strongly. He claimed that in
Mark 13 the readers are being instructed to flee Jerusalem at the time
of the Jewish war, before the actual fall of the city, and to assemble
in Galilee to await the parousia, and similarly 14:28 and 16:7 point to
the imminent expectation of the parousia in Galilee.[52] There are howeve
two problems here. In the first place it is difficult to accept Mark
13 as directing the reader to flee to Galilee. Galilee is nowhere mentioned in the chapter and, more important, the events described, world
wide catastrophes, the cosmos shattering nature of the coming of the
Son of Man, are such as to make it difficult to associate with one explicit geographical location that climactic coming of the Son of Man.

Marxsen's view as to Galilee as a geographical location has been
challenged in his own scholarly tradition where J. Schreiber returns
to a thesis originally presented by Lohmeyer that Galilee for Mark is
the "Galilee of the Gentiles" of Matt. 4:15 and Isa. 8:23 and must be
held to include the Decopolis and the region of Tyre and Sidon (Mark
7:31).[53] But in all of this the references are still geographical, and

all that is being done is to widen them to include areas not in Galilee
in Mark's day. In England, however, by the time Marxsen wrote his Mark
the Evangelist and his fellow Germans commented on it an alternative
and much more promising position had been worked out: the references
to Galilee in 14:28 and 16:7 are references to the Gentile mission.
Here three works are important; none apparently noted by Marxsen or his
critics: R. H. Lightfoot, "appendix" to his Gospel Message of St. Mark
(1950); G. H. Boobyer, "Galilee and Galileans in St. Mark's Gospel,"
BJRL 35 (1952-53), 334-348; C. F. Evans, "I will go before you into Galilee" JTS N. S. 5 (1954), 3-18.

Lightfoot abandoned his original agreement with Lohmeyer that Mark
looked forward to a parousia in Galilee as a geographical location and
reconsidered the whole question of Galilee and the disciples in the gospel of Mark. By analysing the movement of thought (what literary critics would call the "plot") in the gospel as a whole, he shows that for
Mark, Galilee is the place where Jesus worked until his rejection and
thereafter where his disciples worked in his name. But despite the disciples' mission, which Mark does not report as a success!, they understand him no better than the Galileans who had rejected him and Mark
builds up to an impressive climax of total rejection of Jesus by the
disciples and Peter. "The teaching of this gospel seems to be that
nothing short of the Lord's death and resurrection, whereby he overcomes
all resistance and is henceforth united indissolubly with his disciples,
will enable them to understand him and to do his work."[54] So the references to Galilee in 14:28 and 16:7 are such "that the reader's thought
is turned back to the story of the ministry in the early chapters of

he book, and he perceives that this is also the ministry to be fulfil-
ed henceforth by the Lord...in and through his disciples who now repre-
ent him in the world."[55]

This argument from the "plot of the gospel" is impressive and it
as reinforced by Evans, who developed the argument a stage further by
xact exegesis of 14:28. In the first place he pointed out 14:28 is
inked by Mark to 14:27 and the alla with which it begins is adversative,
o Jesus' going into Galilee is the reverse of the smiting of the shep-
erd and the dispersal of the flock. Then he pointed to the fact that
roagein with a personal object means "to lead," especially in Mark
10:32). This then continues the pastoral metaphor and implies that
esus is to lead the disciples to their work in the Gentile world,
alilee (of the Gentiles) being a symbol for the Gentile mission of the
hurch. 14:28 and 16:7 then means that "he is leading you to the Gen-
iles; it is there that you will see him."[56]

Between Lightfoot and Evans, Boobyer had established the fact that
or Mark, Galilee is indeed "Galilee of the Gentiles" and that the whole
ospel witnesses to a special interest in Gentiles. He called attention
o Isa. 8:23-9:6, where in a notable addition to the MT the LXX appar-
ntly claims that God will pour forth the light of his salvation upon
Galilee of the Gentiles," and to Ezek. 47:1-12, where the river of life
lows from Jerusalem towards Galilee. In addition to this the Galilee
f the first century was notably Gentile in ethnic composition and these
wo things may well have led Mark to look upon Galilee "as a natural
tarting place for the Gentile mission."[57] Boobyer argues further that
ark exhibits a special interest in the conversion of the Gentiles,

explicitly in 12:9; 13:10, 27; 14:9 and implicitly in 1:17; 4:32; 10:45; 11:17; 14:24 and elsewhere. Moreover, Mark is at pains to stress the rejection of Jesus by the leadership of Judaism, and hence by the Jewish nation: 3:22; 7:1; 14:10, 11, 43; 14:43; 15:11 (I would add here the redactional concern for the Sanhedrin in the third prediction and in the trial before the High Priest). Side by side with this Mark stresses the necessary corollary, divine judgment upon the Jews: 11:14; 12:9; 13:2; 15:38. Boobyer goes on to develop other aspects of Mark's concern for the Gentiles and his stress on the movement of the gospel from Judaism to the Gentile world, but we have reported enough to show that the case is convincing: Mark does indeed have a special interest in "Galilee of the Gentiles" and in the Gentile mission.

The difficulty with Boobyer's work is not that he does not prove his case, but rather that he is still too much under the influence of a historicizing approach to the gospel of Mark. For Boobyer, Mark's interest in Galilee is as the place for the beginning of the Gentile mission; he neglects the fact that Mark is addressing his own readers directly and that his concern is not to inform them about their own past, as products of the Gentile mission, but to prepare them for an event in their own future, the parousia. This is in a sense symptomatic of this English work altogether for its strength is certainly that it establishes the fact that for Mark "Galilee" has the symbolic meaning of "wherever the mission of the church is carried on"; and we can add to this the obvious fact that for him also the mission of the church post-Easter and the mission of Jesus, pre-Easter, are one and the same thing, and the one therefore, can be talked about in terms of

the other. So that 14:28 and 16:7 refer to the Gentile mission is clear
enough, but the weakness of this work is that it tends to lose the
reference to the parousia in these sayings. Evans indeed develops a
suggestion originally made by Lohmeyer that in them the resurrection
is regarded as a transition from one series of eschatological happenings, represented by the ministry and passion of Jesus, to another
series of eschatological happenings, variously represented in the New
Testament as the ascension of Jesus, his exaltation, the preaching of
the gospel or the pouring out of the spirit."[58] Now Lohmeyer in his
commentary explicitly interprets 16:7 of the parousia, but Evans gives
the impression that he is inclined to think of something like the
vision Paul had when he was called as apostle to the Gentiles.[59] However, the parousia reference has to be maintained. Nothing else will
do justice to the language of 16:7 or to the consistent thrust of the
gospel through the passion and resurrection to the parousia. The
Gentile mission is not to be substituted for the parousia, it is to be
regarded as its locale.

The gospel of Mark exhibits a consistent thrust forwards through
the passion and the resurrection to the parousia. The references to
the disciples and to Galilee are a symbolic use of traditional names
and places to represent Mark's audience and the mission in which Mark's
church stands. The mission of the church, the work of Jesus as risen
Lord, will be brought to a climax by the coming of Jesus, as Son of
Man, which coming will be cosmos shattering. The very nature of this
coming, as Mark presents it in the third part of his apocalyptic discourse, is such that it will be experienced by all men everywhere;

whether they are enroute from Jerusalem to Galilee physically, or
whether their journey has been and is the symbolic one from Jerusalem,
the place of the ultimate rejection, to "Galilee" the place of the
current success of Jesus through his disciples, is immaterial. When
the Son of Man comes, one world ends and another and different one
begins. So again, we are face to face with the situation of Mark's
readers. They are in or between "Jerusalem" and "Galilee," they are
disciples who should accept the full consequences of discipleship in
expectation of the coming of Jesus as Son of Man.

C.   The ending of the gospel of Mark

It is not my purpose to rehearse once more the well-known facts
about the current ending of Mark at 16:8. Beginning with Lohmeyer and
Lightfoot and coming down to the current redaction critics, it has been
possible for scholars to make good sense of the gospel in its present
textual form. At the same time it has to be admitted that to end a
book with ephobounto gar is a barbarism without real parallel in the
Hellenistic world. But, on the other hand, there are also real problems
in accounting for the loss of the original ending if the gospel did once
go beyond the verse at which all textual traditions and both Matthew
and Luke have it as ending.

What the structural analysis showed was that the gospel is complete
as it stands, but it did not and cannot rule out the possibility that
there was once an account of the resurrection closely related to the
passion and anticipating the parousia, functioning in the total gospel
as references to the resurrection do in the prediction units. What our
subsequent discussion has shown--and we have been careful not to build

on the present ending of Mark--is that if the gospel did have an ending now lost that ending must have left the readers where the present ending leaves them, acknowledging the resurrection and anticipating the parousia. From our perspective therefore, the present ending can be treated as the real ending without having to take sides on the question of the ephobounto gar.

V.   The Messianic Secret

There is no need for me to argue for extensive Markan literary
activity in connection with the secrecy motif in the gospel. Since
Wrede first argued that the motif was a dogmatic idea in the tradition
prior to Mark and Bultmann then transferred the motif to Mark himself
there has been growing agreement that it is both an element in the tradition and a major literary device of the evangelist himself. However,
there is no comparable agreement as to what Mark means to express by
this device.[60] It is my contention that we can come to understand this
literary device best by examining the gospel from a literary standpoint.

The dramatic highpoint within the gospel itself lies at the end of
chapter 14. There three themes, which run throughout the gospel, the
messianic secret, the reinterpretation of the Son of God christology,
and the misunderstanding of the disciples, all reach their climax. In
the trial before the Sanhedrin, the messianic secret is finally and formally abandoned as Jesus accepts and publicly acknowledges the designation of Son of God. Then that designation is reinterpreted by the last
and hence climactic use of Son of Man in the gospel. Finally, in a
dramatic scene intercalated between the trial itself and its continuation
(15:1) "as soon as it was morning" Peter denies Jesus, breaks down and
weeps. In all of this, i.e., from 14:53 through 15:1, there is strong
evidence of Markan redactional activity[61] but even if it were not the
case there could be no doubt but that the trial narrative and denial
scene are the climactic treatment of themes of great concern to the
evangelist all through the gospel.

The messianic secret ended then when Jesus acknowledges himself

to be Son of God. Where does it begin? It begins with the redactional
summary 1:34 where "he would not permit the demons to speak, because
they knew him." What they knew becomes clear in the Markan transitional
summary 3:7-14 where the unclean spirits cry out "you are the Son of
God" and are ordered not to make him known. With this clear beginning
and the evident climax as our clues, the thread of the secrecy motif is
easy to follow. The next time we find it, we have the remarkable situation that the secret is conspicuous by its absence. In 5:1-20 everything is present except the command to silence! But our previous discussion of the significance of Galilee for Mark helps us to understand
that this is Decapolis and hence Mark's "Galilee of the Gentiles."
Here Mark is simply reflecting the world he is addressing, the world of
the successful Gentile mission of which the confession of Jesus as Son
of God is the central thrust.

The next commands to secrecy have nothing to do with the messianic
secret. In 5:43 Jesus commands secrecy not about his status but about
the resuscitation of the little girl, and in 7:36 it is Jesus' wonder-
working power which creates such an impression that the news of it
bursts the bounds which Jesus himself as the wonder-worker attempted
to set for it. Following L. E. Keck's very persuasive suggestion that
these stories are part of a pre-Markan cycle which presented Jesus as a
theios anēr,[62] we can judge these commands to silence to be part of the
dramatic technique of presenting the power of the wonder-worker in such
stories. In any case, as Bultmann remarks, these commands to secrecy
are different in kind from the messianic secrecy commands of 1:34 and
3:11f.[63]

The Markan thread becomes evident again in 9:9 and 9:30. In 9:9
we have the command to secrecy in regard to the status of Jesus as Son
of God revealed in the transfiguration epiphany, but at this point there
is a significant development: the command to secrecy is to remain in
effect "until the Son of Man should have risen from the dead." Our
structural analysis of the gospel showed that the complex first prediction unit - transfiguration unit was central to the structure of the
narrative leading up to the twin climax of apocalyptic discourse and
passion narrative and it is not surprising therefore that the messianic
secrecy command associated with it should also be a turning point. What
was commanded in general before is now subject to the limitation "until
the Son of Man should have arisen from the dead." We should also note
that it is only after the first prediction unit that such a use of Son
of Man would have made sense. Only now in the movement of the gospel's
"plot" is it possible to use Son of Man and have it carry all the nuances
of meaning Mark intends it to have: authority (2:10, 28), necessary
suffering (8:31), and apocalyptic judgment (8:38). In 9:9 therefore
both the fact of the limitation and the form in which it is expressed
are significant for our interpretation of the messianic secret in the
gospel of Mark.

In 9:30 the secrecy motif appears again but this time explicitly
in connection with the second prediction of the passion and resurrection
of the Son of Man. In view of 9:9 this is not surprising. 9:9 taught
us that there is an intimate connection between the necessity for
secrecy about Jesus as Son of God and the passion and resurrection of
Jesus as Son of Man. Now in 9:30 there is dramatic secrecy about the

very presence of Jesus, in order that he may instruct his disciples concerning this mystery. Mark 9:30-32 in fact gives the impression of <u>movement</u>, by setting the command to secrecy in the context of a journey through Galilee, and this is as it should be. After 9:9 the stage has been set for the formal giving up of the secret in 14:62 and it is fitting therefore that the one reference to the secret between these two high points is a transitional one.

By his use of the literary device of the messianic secret Mark therefore first calls his readers' attention to the fact that the demons knew Jesus as Son of God. This they, and he, would accept readily since such a thing was part of their realistic understanding of the world and the forces at work in it. Mark himself has been taught by Jesus as risen Lord that to understand him as Son of God, one has to interpret that concept by means of the nuances that can only be expressed by a development of the Son of Man symbolism: authority and suffering. So he next goes on to depict Jesus as instructing the disciples in this, and as stressing its necessity by refusing to allow Son of God to be applied to him until the conditions are such that it can be used properly. When the narrative has reached the point where these conditions are fulfilled, Jesus accepts the designation and gives it its final reinterpretation, and Peter symbolizes the failure to understand--and its consequences--in the denial scene. The messianic secret is a literary device made necessary by the fact that Mark is using narrative for a didactic purpose, and it is a means designed to achieve that purpose more effectively. How far this is conscious literary artistry on the part of the evangelist and how far it is an instinctive follow-

ing out of the consequences of the fact that for Mark the ministry of
Jesus before and after the resurrection is one and the same ministry
we cannot say.

VI. The Purpose of the Evangelist

The gospel of Mark is written in the form of narrative, and in particular in the form of realistic narrative. For all that he inherits miracle stories in which Jesus was represented as a wonder-working theios anēr, and for all that he stresses the power and authority of Jesus, Mark presents Jesus as a man among men. The Jesus of Mark's gospel is subject to the plotting of his enemies; he is presented as a carpenter who can be rejected, and whose power can be frustrated by unbelief. He can be "moved with pity" by the condition of a leper, and he can be moved to anger by constant importunity, "O faithless genera-tion, how long am I to bear with you?" Under stress he can react almost despairingly, "My God, my God, why hast thou forsaken me?" Similarly Peter is presented in very human terms. Indeed, in his discussion of the representation of reality in western literature E. Auerbach takes Mark's account of the denial of Jesus by Peter as a prime example of realism in narrative.[64] So impressed is he by the realism that he assumes--wrongly--that Peter's personal account is the basis of the story.

In this regard we may compare the very different presentation of Jesus in John's gospel, or of Peter in the Acts of the Apostles. In John we do not have realistic narrative but rather something like the scenario for a sacred oratorio,[65] and in Acts we have something much nearer to the religious propaganda of the Hellenistic world as Peter brings Ananias to death or Simon Magus to penitence.

It was the realism of Mark's narrative which helped to convince nineteenth century scholarship of the historicity of the gospel. "If

all other arguments against the mythic origin of the evangelic narratives were wanting, this vivid and simple record, stamped with the most
distinct impress of independence and originality...would be sufficient
to refute a theory subversive of all faith in history." So B. F. West-
cott writing against D. F. Strauss in 1851;[66] and we saw above that
Auerbach assumed personal reminiscence behind the story of Peter's
denial of Jesus. Today we would account for this Markan realism in
other ways--the controlling influence of the passion, the presentation
of Peter in terms of failure and misunderstanding, the extensive use of
wisdom-type materials, and so on--but the point is not that we must
account for it but that we must understand its effect.

Narrative, a story, has the effect of catching the reader up into
the action, of involving him in the plot; the reader or hearer is drawn
into the middle of the drama. But a necessary prerequisite of this is
the ability of the reader--or hearer, the distinction is unreal--to
identify himself with the characters or to picture himself in the circumstances depicted in the story. So, for example, certain of the
parables of Jesus have an extraordinary ability to reach successive
generations of readers because their circumstances are universally
human. So long as men live in families they can be caught up into the
story of the Prodigal Son, and so long as they must travel through
dangerous territory they will applaud the Good Samaritan. The fact
that crisis is a constituent element of all human life gives the story
of the Unjust Steward universal effectiveness--except where stern
moralizing forbids the appreciation of a picaresque rogue, as in the
case of the author(s) of Luke 16:8b and 9! But where the circumstances

or characters are foreign--where, so to speak, the furniture of the
story is strange--then the reader is not affected in the same way by
it. Where the processes of agriculture are no longer a matter of
immediate experience, and where the comparative success of failure of
any given harvest is not literally a matter of life and death, the
parable of the Sower loses its power, as that of the Lost Sheep loses
its point when the loss of one sheep is not a real catastrophe.

We are on the way to appreciating the effect of Mark's narrative
upon the readers for which it was written. By no doubt unconscious
artistry it is a fine example of realistic or mimetic narrative and
as such had, and has, the ability to catch the reader up into the story.
As we have seen this was in fact Mark's intent. In the gospel Jesus
directly addresses Mark's readers, and not only in the apocalyptic discourse; the characters (except for Jesus) are representations of indi-
viduals Mark is addressing; the teaching which Jesus gives is directed
towards the actual situation and problems of the Markan church, and so
on.

The most important thing about the evangelist Mark, in this particular context, is that he is the last and greatest representative of
that dynamic impulse in earliest Christianity to conceptualize one's
own experience, understanding and circumstances in the form of sayings
of the pre-Easter Jesus and of stories of his ministry in Galilee and
Judea. So early Christian prophets created apocalyptic Son of Man
sayings in the form of sayings of Jesus; early Christian scribes could
develop their exegesis of scripture in the form of Jesus debating with
opponents and teaching his disciples; and early Christian communities

could express their struggles with their fellow Jews in the form of
controversy stories between Jesus and scribes, Pharisees or Sadducees.
This is the tradition in which Mark stands and he exploits the poten-
tiality to great effect, gathering, redacting, even freely creating
material in the form of Jesus tradition to express his own convictions
and concerns. But Mark took a step none of his predecessors had taken,
for all that there was preparation for it in the tradition; he put his
material together in the form of a coherent story with a beginning in
Galilee, a middle in Caesarea Philippi and a climax in Jerusalem. The
nature of the material he was using and his purpose in using it was
such that the result was mimetic narrative and this fact created a
possibility that had not been there before: the possibility of involving his readers in the gospel story as a whole rather than in some
particular part of it, such as a controversy story, the Lord's Supper
paradosis, or even a connected passion narrative. The nature of this
no doubt unconsciously created form was such that it did in fact catch
up the reader, lead him from Galilee through Caesarea Philippi to
Jerusalem, and leave him standing with the women at the empty tomb.

Let me pause for a moment to stress the fact that I am not claiming for the evangelist Mark the deliberately reflective genius of a
Shakespeare, a Henry Fielding or a James Joyce. He no doubt moved in
part by unconscious response to a particular challenge and the potential
within a tradition to meet it. Above all he must have been responding
almost instinctively to the needs he saw out of a conviction that
Jesus was leading him forward in "Galilee" and that the ministry of his
church was that of Jesus in that Galilee. But the fact remains that

he moment was almost explosively creative, that the form he created,
owever unconsciously, was such as to meet dramatically the need for
hich he created it. Had it not been then it would not have had the im-
act it did have in the churches, there would have been no gospels of
Matthew and Luke, and the history of early Christian litereature would
ave been very different, as would the make-up of the New Testament.

To return to the evangelist Mark and his purpose, we are now in a
osition to state that purpose both as it is revealed in a structural
nalysis of the gospel and in a consideration of the gospel as in fact
eing in the form of mimetic narrative. Mark's purpose is to catch the
attention of his readers and lead him from Galilee through Caesarea
Philippi to Jerusalem and the empty tomb, and to the realization that
he, the reader, is being challenged to discipleship in the context of
the prospect of the coming of Jesus as Son of Man.

In connection with this main purpose there are at least two related
subsidiary or auxiliary purposes: the christological and that of the
discipleship parenesis. Christologically Mark is concerned to combat a
false christology, most probably of the theios anēr type, and this he
does particularly by his use of Son of Man and by his conscious sub-
ordination of the story of Jesus to the passion. Then on the basis of
this he turns to the discipleship parenesis which is the climactic
feature of each of the three prediction units.

We believe that insofar as these points are not an expression of a
general scholarly consensus we have argued them in this paper. Now by
way of conclusion we turn to a brief discussion of the structure and purpose of Luke-Acts as this contrasts with that of Mark and so helps to
set Mark in perspective.

VII. The Structure and Purpose of Luke-Acts

The most striking thing about Luke-Acts as compared to Mark is, of course, the very existence of Acts; the fact that the one volume gospel has become a two volume work: a gospel and an account of the spread of the Good News from Jerusalem to Rome. Luke has set the two volumes carefully in relationship to one another by the literary device of stressing the movement of the Spirit. He redacts the Markan account of the baptism of Jesus so that it is no longer a baptism but an account of the descent of the spirit upon Jesus. The reference to the baptism is now one of a series of clauses setting the stage for the action of the main verbs, the opening of the heavens and the descent of the spirit. Then at the account of the crucifixion the Markan, "Jesus uttered a loud cry, and breathed his last" becomes, in Luke, "Jesus, crying with a loud voice, said, 'Father, into thy hands I commit my spirit!' and having said this he breathed his last." Then in Acts the descent of the spirit at Pentecost is interpreted as a baptims, Acts 1:8, and as is well known the spirit functions as strongly in the narrative of Acts as it does in that of the gospel of Luke. So the descent and activity of the spirit sets the two narratives in a parallel relationship to one another. Significantly, there is no ascent of the spirit at the end of Acts; there cannot be, because Luke conceives of the era of the spirit as continuing into his own day.

The major modifications by Luke of the structure of the gospel of Mark are the addition of birth stories and an account of the resurrection and ascension, and the introduction of the loosely knit travel narrative, Luke 9:51-18:14. We concentrate for the moment on the travel narrative. This begins, "When the days drew near for his ascension, he (Jesus) set his face to go to Jerusalem." In other words, Luke signals the movement of the plot of his story to its climax by the literary device of a mental resolve on the part of its chief protagonist. Now this is a common enough literary device, and what is not often noted is that Luke does the same thing in Acts, Acts 19:21: "Paul resolved in the spirit to...go to Jerusalem, saying, 'After I have been there, I must also see Rome'." From this point forward in Acts we have the same loosely knit kind of travel narrative until Paul arrives in Rome that we have in the gospel from 9:51 until Jesus arrives in Jerusalem. In both cases therefore we have no doubt of the intent of Luke: his first volume is to end at Jerusalem with the ascension, and his second with Paul in Rome.

The movement from Jerusalem to Rome is the theme of the second volume; this is clear not only from the resolve of the two protagonists but also from the final words of Jesus as risen Lord to his disciples, (Acts 1:8) with their geographical movement Jerusalem, Judea, Samaria, end of the earth (i.e., Rome). This theme is maintained also in the case of the apostle Paul. Against all historical probability Luke has him begin his witness in Jerusalem, (Acts 9:27-29), have his commissioning trance in Jerusalem, (Acts 22:17-21), (n.b. "I will send you far away to the Gentiles:", i.e., to Rome), and again witness in Jerusalem, (Acts 26:20), where it is first Damascus, then Jerusalem, Judea and to the Gentiles. The fact that each of the three accounts of Paul's commissioning sounds this same note is an indication of its importance for Luke.

The narratives both in the gospel and in Acts are mimetic in the sense in which I am using that word. Luke's readers would have no problems in identifying with them and being caught up into them. Indeed Luke goes to considerable pains to build bridges between his narratives and the characters in them on the one hand, and his readers on the other. His Jesus is immensely attractive, as the piety of centuries attests, and he has the human traits of compassion and of needing to get away by himself, as well as being a paradigm of human religious behaviour, attending the synagogue "as his custom was," resorting to prayer at the great moments of crisis in his life, and so on. Peter, Stephen, Philip and Paul in Acts are heroic characters but not so much so as to prevent the readers from identifying with them, from being cuaght up into the heroic age of the church. Again, they engage in religious activity which would have a correspondence in the life of the Lukan church: they baptize and lay on hands, and the gift of the spirit follows; they pray, and they receive guidance through dreams and visions. So the purpose of Luke, and the effect of his writing, is to lead his readers from Nazareth to Jerusalem, and from Jerusalem to Rome. When the reader stands with Paul in Rome and hears the preaching and the teaching "quite openly and unhindered" then Luke's prupose is achieved. The drama has reached its climax, the faith has a new centre, and the Christian can stand fast in his tradition and continue the witness in the world.

It can be seen that there are real differences between the purpose of the narrative of Luke and that of Mark. Where Mark leaves his reader on the way to "Galilee" and in expectation of the parousia, Luke leaves

-59-

his in Rome with the anticipation of a continuing witness in the world.
But there is a further difference between Luke and Mark, again percep-
tible in Luke's modifications of Mark's structure. Where Mark involves
his readers directly in his story--addressing them out of it, reflecting
their situation in it, and so on--Luke separates his readers from the
story of Jesus and then provides a new and more formal way of relating
them to it. Mark's gospel is open ended so that the reader relates
directly to it; Luke's is closed off so that the reader relates to it
more formally. To this end Luke adds a beginning, the birth narratives,
to Mark and in this way gives the story of Jesus an end which separates
his readers from it. Then he begins the story his readers are directly
involved in, the story of their church, with the baptism-return of the
spirit narrative of Pentecost.

Between Mark and Luke there has been a fundamental change of attitude to the narrative of the ministry of Jesus. Mark, as I argued
earlier, still stands in the tradition of earlier days when there was
direct identification between the ministry of Jesus and that of the
church and the one was talked about in terms of the other. But once a
gospel is written the attitude begins to change, the narrated gospel
is a story with a beginning, a middle and an end, and as such introduces
a separation, a dividing line, between what it relates and the coninua-
tion in the life of the church. So it becomes possible and indeed
inevitable to think of the ministry of Jesus as distinct from that of
the risen Lord and to reflect upon the ministry of Jesus as having a
climax--so Mark--and then as having an end--so the church after Mark.
Of course, it is not simply the fact of the writing of Mark's gospel

which caused the change. The change was already in progress and the writing of Mark was probably as much an effect as a cause of the change. But the fact remains that Mark did write a story with a deliberately open-ended climax whereas the effect of reading that story inevitably is to change the climax into an ending, and then to envisage a separate beginning. This is what Luke does, but that it was in any case inevitable can be seen from the fact that Matthew also does it, for the effect of the Great Commission is to end the ministry of Jesus and to begin a separate and distinct ministry of the church. In recent scholarly discussion this matter has been discussed in terms of the Lukan Heilsgeschichte and of the question as to whether Matthew has a similar understanding. I am addressing myself to the matter from the standpoint of a literary crictical understanding of narratives, but in my terms I am reaching a position similar to that which Bornkamm and Strecker express in theirs.[67]

   To stay with Luke, we can see the new attitude to the narrated ministry of Jesus in the prologues to the gospel and to Acts. The ministry of Jesus is now seen as "the things which have been accomplishe among us," Luke 1:1, and it has become important to deal with "all that Jesus did and taught," Acts 1:1 NEB, because now the time of Jesus has become a kind of sacred time separated from the time of the reader, although determinative for it. Now the reader relates to a sacred whole which is separate from his own experience, however closely he may relate to it through the channels provided by Luke and his church, while earlier the experience of the reader was at one with, and indeed part of the sacred time.

This difference between Mark and Luke (and Matthew also) is of
real importance for the interpretation of the gospel of Mark. For all
they are the three synoptic evangelists, if Mark is an evangelist then
Matthew and Luke are something else for there is the fundamental difference in attitude to the narrative of the ministry to which we have
called attention. In some respects Mark is closer to John of Patmos
than he is to Luke and Matthew. Like Mark, John of Patmos, has a central symbol, the Lamb, of whom it is important that he has suffered;
like him he addresses his readers directly. For John his own story and
that of his church is part of that which he narrates, and it is his
intention to confront his reader with the necessity for discipleship
in expectation of the parousia. For all that Mark and John of Patmos
use very different forms there are strong parallels between them in the
way their material functions and in their overall purpose. If Luke and
Matthew are gospels then there are many respects in which Mark is an
apocalypse.

VIII. Towards an Interpretation of the Gospel of Mark

The current hermeneutical discussion is making it clear to us that the interpretation of a text held to be of some significance is no easy matter. There are at least three standpoints from which the meaning of the text has to be explored. There is the standpoint represented by such names as Bultmann, Heidegger, Gadamer and by the "new hermeneutic." The spectrum is broad, but it centers on the fact that there are ways in which a text addresses us directly, challenging our understanding of existence, bringing reality into being for us in language, becoming for us a "word event," and so on. To plagiarize Fuchs, the focus of attention here is upon the way the text interprets us rather than we the text. Something may be said to happen in the text that affects us directly. Then there is the standpoint of historical criticism, which explores the circumstances under which the text was written, the intent of the author, the meaning it had for its intended readers, and all else that is necessary or possible to reach a historical understanding of the text. Finally, there is the standpoint of literary criticism which explores the form of the text and the way such forms function, the language of the text and what can be known of the way such language functions. Of course, these standpoints overlap, the second with the third and the third with the first, but to enumerate them separately is to grasp something of the complexity of the hermeneutical task.

So far as the gospel of Mark is concerned we have made great progress in the matter of historical criticism. Standing as we do at a point where we can utilize the results of source, form and redaction criticism, and avail ourselves of the insights made possible by the

ise and fall of the Markan hypothesis, we can speak with some certainty
s to what the text was intended to say to its readers and what it did
n fact say to them. Indeed we can say so much about these things, and
hese things are so interesting to people who are primarily historians,
s many New Testament scholars are, that the temptation is to think
hat in doing so we are interpreting the text. But such is not the case.
or all that the results of historical criticism are indispensable to the
ermeneutical task, historical criticism is not itself interpretation.
s compared with historical criticism the literary criticism of the
ospel of Mark is in its infancy, as indeed is the case for all the
exts of the New Testament. For years Amos Wilder was almost alone in
ursuing it but his Language of the Gospel: Early Christian Rhetoric
inally opened other eyes as to its importance, and at the same time
ew Testament scholars found themselves on the same faculties as liter-
ry critics and hence by circumstance reached a position Wilder enjoys
y reason of being Wilder! Hence, there is now a growing interest in it,
specially in America, and the intent of this paper has been in part to
ake some contribution to the literary critical study of the gospel of
ark. Whatever may be the merits of my contribution the fact is that
he outlook for this kind of work is very promising and the contribution
t can be expected to make to the hermeneutical task is very considerable.

It is the first standpoint which presents the most difficulties
s we approach the gospel of Mark. Indeed there is a sense in which we
an only stand still and let the gospel approach us! In a sense we can
o little more than wait for the "word event" to happen for us in the
ext of Mark. But that is not enough, for at least two reasons. In the

first place, the experienced guidance of the critic is a great help in
understanding what can happen as a text confronts us. I have myself,
for example recently been confronted by the musical "Hair." That is
certainly a word event in the sense in which the new hermeneutic would
use the term, and there is a sense in which one can only allow oneself
to be swept along by it. But the drama critic understands the how and
the why of it in a way that the outsider does not and I am sure that
for me the "happening" would not have been so intense had I not prepared
myself for it by availing myself of that expert help beforehand. In an
analogous way the critic of the gospel of Mark must help his readers
to approach the text of the gospel with all the preparation possible.
But we are perhaps learning a new humility in realizing that historical
and literary criticism are only prolegomena to the interpretation of the
text and the being interpreted by text. Similarly, of course, an interpretation of the text by a Bultmann, or a Fuchs is also only prolegomena to the interpretation of that text by another reader.

That brings me to the second point I would want to make in this
context. In the last analysis, the interpretation of being interpreted
by a text is a highly personal matter. But that does not mean that it
must be allowed to become so highly subjective that anything may be
read into a text that a given reader wishes to find in it. Even in the
context of the "new hermeneutic"--perhaps especially in that context!
--we have to maintain the distinction between exegesis and eisegesis.
Here the historical and literary critic can be of real help for he can
establish the guidelines of the original intent and natural function
of the text. While these perhaps can be no more than guidelines they

are nonetheless to be respected in that they are indications of what is
actually inherent in the text itself as distinct from what can be read
into that text by the use of an undisciplined imagination. There is
after all a sense in which we are always dealing with a discrete text
as a concrete actuality.

Even when we have considered the historical and literary criticism
of a text, and the insights of the philosopher of language, we have
still not yet reached the end of the complexities involved in the interpretation of the particular text of the gospel of Mark. In addition
to being a "text held to be of some significance" this gospel is also
a religious text, and in addition to that it is a Christian religious
text. This introduces a fourth and a fifth factor into our discussion
because it means that we have to consider the insights of the historian
of religion, whose profession it is to study the form and function of
religious texts, and of the historian of Christian thought--perhaps,
better, the historian of Christian hermeneutics--who concerns himself
with the role which Christian religious texts have played in Christian
history, thought and experience. Both of these groups of insights can
be expected to help us in the task of interpreting the gospel of Mark
and both will have to be taken seriously into account. At the same
time neither is going to supply the key which will solve all our problems because there are limitations to the use of both in connection with
a given text.

The historian of religion must necessarily concern himself with
the general rather than with the particular, with what a text has in
common with other texts rather than with what is unique to that text

itself. It is of course essential both to take into account what a text
has in common with other texts and also to learn what it is that is
distinctive about the particular text. In the case of the gospel of
Mark the historian of religion would readily recognize the presentation of Jesus as a miracle working theios anēr in the cycle of stories
isolated by L. E. Keck, which we discussed above, but then he would
have to go on to recognize that in Mark these stories are being used in
a quite particular way, namely to correct the christology originally
expressed in them. To take another example, W. A. Beardslee has recently pointed out that the gospels combine in themselves two distinct
traits which the historian of religion recognizes as functions of religious narrative: "The reenactment of the past and the leading into the
future." But in contrast with other religious narratives the gospels,
and I would add "especially the gospel of Mark," tend to grapple with
the issues of life less in mythological terms and more in terms of concrete personal existences.[68] Our discussion above indicated the reason
for this: the particular and perhaps in a history of religions context
almost unique use of the Jesus symbol in the synoptic tradition and by
the evangelist Mark. Another way of getting at this particular point
would be to say that in no Hellenistic religious cult does the founder
figure play the role that Jesus plays in the gospels. In this respect
Pauline Christianity, with its total lack of any interest in the founder
figure beyond that of his mythologically conceived death and resurrection as the redeemer, is much more readily recognizable to the historian of Hellenistic religion than is the gospel of Mark. But then we
have to remind ourselves that the gospel of Mark is also a product of

Hellenistic Christianity.

It can be seen that the insights of the historian of religion are essential to the interpretation of the gospel of Mark, even if they are not the ultimate key to it. The same thing can and must be said about the insights of the historian of Christian hermeneutics. Actually, of the books in the New Testament the gospel of Mark is perhaps the least affected by this particular aspect of our hermeneutical concern. Through the centuries Mark has been regarded as "merely the lackey and abbreviator of Matthew,"[69] and so comparatively neglected. Indeed almost the only significant statement about the evangelist Mark to come to us from the tradition of the ancient church is that he was the hermeneutēs Petrou (Papias quoting the "elder"), and that we now know to be meaningless in our context. Analysis of the material in the gospel shows that it is in no part derived from the reminiscences of Peter, pace V. Taylor and many other commentators. After Papias almost the next really significant statement about the gospel of Mark comes from nineteenth century scholarship with its "Markan hypothesis," whereby it was maintained that Mark was both the earliest gospel and also largely historical in nature. Again analysis of the material in the gospel shows that this is not the case. Although Mark is earlier than either Matthew or Luke he is not thereby any more historical than they; as a matter of fact he has much less interest in what we would call history than has Luke. The Markan hypothesis proceeded from the mistaken assumption that the synoptic tradition was fundamentally historical reminiscence with an overlay of legendary accretion and dogmatic rein-terpretation. But more recent research has shown that this is simply not the case. From the very beginning, as we pointed out above, the synoptic tradition was a-historical, if by historical one means to imply a concern for Jesus "as he actually was."

We are in the position, therefore, of urging that the history of the interpretation of the gospel of Mark in the church has to be taken seriously, but then of claiming that the two most important interpretations of that gospel in the church are in fact fundamentally mistaken in that they are untrue to the actual nature of the text itself! Here two things need to be said. In the first place, the history of the interpretation of the gospel of Mark in the church is by no means typical of that of New Testament texts as a whole. From Papias to the rise of the Markan hypothesis the gospel of Mark was comparatively neglected by the church; hence we do not have the rich history of its interpretation with accompanying insights that we would have in the case, for example, of the gospel of Matthew or the letter to the Romans. Then, secondly, I am myself consciously ascribing normative influence to the results of historical criticism. Papias and the Markan hypothesis are both "mistaken" because what they have to say is not in fact born out by a historical critical investigation of that text. Implicit here is the claim that where historical criticism can establish the original, historical meaning and purpose of the text this meaning and purpose is to be regarded as normative, and subsequent translations of that meaning and purpose into the idioms of other generations and situations may not do violence to it. The difference between exegesis and eisegesis is structly to be observed!

So it is that I would argue that in the case of the gospel of

Mark one has to take seriously into account five separate aspects of the hermeneutical task: historical criticism, literary criticism, the philosophy of language, the insights of the historian of religion, and those of the historian of Christian hermeneutics. But where there is conflict the first of these should exercise normative influence and control over the others.

FOOTNOTES

1. R. S. Crane, The Language of Criticism and the Structure of Poetry (Toronto: University of Toronto Press, 1953), p. 146.

2. I use Mark and Luke to designate both the gospels and the evange-lists, adding a further definition only where necessary for clarity or emphasis.

3. V. Taylor, The Gospel according to Saint Mark. London: Macmillan, 1953.

4. Darmstadt: Wissenschaftliche Buchgesellschaft, 1964 (=1919).

5. The insight that such summaries are essentially transitional in nature rather than simply either beginning or ending a section of the gospel I owe to a student of mine, Vernon Robbins, The Christo-logy of Mark (University of Chicago Divinity School dissertation, 1969), pp. 56-60.

6. On 13:1-5a as the introduction to the discourse and as Markan composition see J. Lambrecht, Die Redaktion der Markus-Apokalypse (Rome: Pontifical Biblical Institute, 1967), pp. 68-91. Mark 14: 1-2, 10-12 is probably traditional, the intercalation of the Bethany incident being Markan. Such intercalation is a well recognized characteristic of the evangelist's compositional technique, often used by him for narrative, dramatic or interpre-tative reasons, as here. T. A. Burkill, Mysterious Revelation (Ithaca: University of Cornell Press, 1963), p. 121 n. 10; D. E. Nineham, Saint Mark (Harmondsworth: Penguin Books, 1963), pp. 370-3.

7. M. Dibelius, From Tradition to Gospel (trans. B. L. Wolf; New York: Scribner's, 1935), p. 115 notes that "the prophecy of suffering introduced by Mark at 8:31 has obviously covered over the conclusion to the passage."

8. W. Wrede, Das Messiasgeheimnis in den Evengelien (Göttingen: Vandenhoeck & Ruprecht, 1901), p. 91.

9. Mark, p. 377.

10. In this respect the position of J. Jeremias is perhaps particularly important. In a personal letter to me responding to my contribution to his Festschrift, "The Use of (para)didonai in Connection with the Passion of Jesus in the New Testament," in E. Lohse (ed.), Der Ruf Jesu und die Antwort der Gemeinde (Göttingen: Vandenhoeck & Ruprecht, 1970), pp. 204-212, Professor Jeremias pointed out that Mark 9:31 exhibits an obvious seam in that there is a change of tense between the first part of the saying and the second: "The Son of Man is delivered...they will kill him..." The Son of Man saying could well have been received by the community from Jesus as a mashal (mysterious saying) and have formed the basis for the development of the (para)didonai tradition and hence ultimately of the passion predictions. His point about the obvious seam in Mark 9:31 is well taken and it makes it clear that 9:31a is traditional and pre-Markan. As to whether it goes back to Jesus, this is a question which would require a discussion quite beyond the confines of this paper. It will be seen below that the change of tense admirably serves the Markan compositional purpose.

11. *Tradition*, p. 226.

12. *Ibid.*

13. E. Lohmeyer, *Das Evangelium des Markus* (Göttingen: Vandenhoeck & Ruprecht, 1937), pp. 164f.

14. H. E. Tödt, *The Son of Man in the Synoptic Tradition* (trans. D. M. Barton; London: S.C.M. Press, 1965), pp. 152-221.

15. *Ibid.*, p. 202.

16. F. Hahn, *The Titles of Jesus in Christology* (trans. H. Knight and G. Ogg; London: Lutterworth Press, 1969), pp. 37-42.

17. "The Passion and Resurrection Predictions in Mark's Gospel," *Interpretation* 22 (1968), 421-42. German original, *ZTK* 64 (1967), 16-39.

18. J. Schreiber, *Theologie des Vertrauens* (Hamburg: Furche-Verlag, 1967), p. 106 makes the point that the "after three days" is found only in Mark and that this fact demands that we ask first if it has a special meaning "im Rahmen seiner Gesamtredaktion."

19. *Interp.* 22 (1968), 425f.

20. *Son of Man*, p. 196.

21. N. Perrin, *What is Redaction Critcism?* (Philadelphia: Fortress Press, 1969), pp. 44-51; "The Composition of Mark 9:1," *Novum Testamentum* 11 (1969), 67-70.

22. Attempts to recover a pre-Markan form of the Caesarea Philippi pericope have been unsuccessful. Schreiber contends that vss. 27-29, 31, 32b-33 are pre-Markan but the evidence is of such a nature that he has to argue that "the fact that the style of the pericope is Markan can support our proposal that underlying it is a

coextensive pre-Markan tradition." Interp. 22 (1968), 436. In an
earlier day and different context the late T. W. Manson used to
describe that kind of argument as "heads I win, tails you lose!"

23. N. Perrin, "The Creative Use of Son of Man by Mark," Union Seminary
Quarterly Review 23 (1967/68), 357-65; "The Christology of Mark:
a Study in Methodology," Journal of Religion.

24. For what follows see my article "The Use of (para)didonai in the
New Testament in connection with the Passion of Jesus," publication
details in note 10 above.

25. K. G. Kuhn, "Jesus in Gethsemane," Evangelische Theologie 12
(1952/53), pp. 260-85.

26. One cannot distinguish between didonai and paradidonai in the Koine.

27. That Mark 9:12b is an insertion into an already completed text of
Mark was argued by Lohmeyer, Markus, p. 183 n. 1 and by R. Bult-
mann, History of the Synoptic Tradition (trans. J. Marsh; Oxford:
Basil Blackwell, rev. ed., 1968), p. 125.

28. Strecker, Interp. 22 (1968), 425.

29. See the quote from Strecker in n. 16 above.

30. Lohmeyer, Markus, p. 8.

31. Again following Lohmeyer as I did earlier on this point.
See n. 13 above.

32. A statement such as Schreiber's (Theologie des Vertrauens, p. 127)
that Mark 13 is prior to the passion narrative and hence subordinate to it is dependent upon a too ready acceptance of the dictum
that the gospel is a passion narrative with an extended introduction
(Kähler) and is not born out by the structural analysis of the text.

33. R. H. Lightfoot, The Gospel Message of St. Mark (Oxford: O.U.P.,
1950), pp. 48-59. More recently L. Gaston, No Stone on Another
(Leiden: E. J. Brill, 1970), 478f. Some of the parallels are as
follows. In 13:9 Christians will be delivered up (paradidonai),
beaten and made to stand before governors, all of which happens to
Jesus in the passion narrative. The use of the Roman four watch
system in 13:35 parallels the time references in 14:17, 41, 72;
15:1. 13:26 and 14:62 are both references to the coming of the
Son of Man.

34. A recent suggestion by J. Schreiber is that the transfiguration
anticipates the exaltation of Jesus at his cross, and in support
of this it is argues that the "after six days" of 9:2 corresponds
to the time span of the Markan passion narrative: 1st. day:
11:1-11; 2nd.: 11:12-19; 3rd.: 11:20-13:37; 4th. and 5th.:
14:1-11; 6th.: 14:12-72; 7th.: 15:1-47. Schreiber, Theologie,
pp. 109, 119-20. This is a step forward in that it takes the six
day reference in 9:2 seriously but it seems unlikely that so
important a point would be made by Mark by means of such a very
indistinct chronology of the passion. Only the first three days
are at all clearly marked, and that there are six to be counted
has been rejected by Lohmeyer, Markus, pp. 227-8, and E. Haenchen,
Der Weg Jesu (Berlin: A. Töpelmann, 1966), p. 373 n. 1, among
others.

35. E. g. Bultmann, Tradition, p. 260.

36. E. g. Burkill, Mysterious Revelation, p. 158 n. 14.

37. Werner H. Kelber (a student of mine), The Kingdom and the Parousia

in the Gospel of Mark (University of Chicago Divinity School
dissertation, 1970), p. 64: "Rather than identifying the resurrection with the transfiguration 9:9 defines the resurrection as
the terminus post quem of the fulfillment of Jesus' epiphany."
Kelber's dissertation is a full scale redaction critical investigation of the eschatology of Mark and I am indebted to it at a
number of points, especially in connection with the transfiguration, with Mark 13, and in the criticism of Schreiber's Theologie
des Vertrauens.

38. W. Marxsen, Mark the Evangelist (trans. R. A. Harrisville; New York
and Nashville: Abingdon Press, 1969 [German original, 1956]),
pp. 151-206. Subsequent major studies include the following:
H. Conzelmann, "Geschichte und Eschaton nach Mc 13," ZNW 50 (1959),
210-21.
L. Hartman, Prophecy Interpreted. The Formation of Some Jewish
Apocalyptic Texts and of the Eschatological Discourse Mark 13 par.
Lund: C. W. K. Gleerup, 1966.
J. Lambrecht, Die Redaktion der Markus-Apokalypse (n. 5 above),
1967.
R. Pesch, Naherwartungen. Tradition and Redaktion in Mk 13.
Düsseldorf: Patmos-Verlag, 1968.
L. Gaston, No Stone on Another (n. 31 above [1970]), pp. 8-64.
W. H. Kelber, The Kingdom and the Parousia (n. 35 above [1970]),
pp. 139-184.

39. Marxsen, Mark, p. 167.

40. Conzelmann, ZNW 50 (1959), 220 n. 50.

41. Mark, p. 183.

42. ZNW 50 (1959), 219-21.

43. Gaston, No Stone, pp. 57f.

44. The point is perhaps comparatively unimportant but I hold the view that vss. 2, 4 indicate the situation after the fall of Jerusalem and the destruction of the temple. In any case what matters is that the situation of the Jewish War and consequently of heightened apocalytic expectation is involved.

45. Kelber, Kingdom and Parousia, pp. 158ff.

46. Gaston, No Stone, p. 13.

47. Two typical representatives of the possibilities would be Taylor, Mark, p. 608, that the reference is to a resurrection appearance and Lohmeyer, Markus, pp. 355f. that it is to the parousia. R. H. Lightfoot first held Lohmeyer's position, Locality and Doctrine in the Gospels (New York: Harper and Bros., n. d. [1938]), pp. 52-65, 73-7, but later changed his mind and argued for a reference to the Gentile mission, Gospel Message, pp. 106-16. In this latter position he was supported by his pupil, C. F. Evans, "I will go before you into Galilee," JTS N.S. 5 (1954), 3-18. This third possibility will be discussed further in our text, immediately below.

48. Lightfoot, Locality and Doctrine, p. 76.

49. That 14:28 and 16:7 are redactional has been demonstrated by Marxsen, Mark, pp. 74-81.

50. The references are in n. 47 above.

51. Schreiber's thesis is dubious for a number of reasons. In the first

place its point of departure is a questionable analysis of the
Markan account of the crucifixion; an analysis questionable not
least because it ascribes to two very different sources the same
homogenous use of the Old Testament, especially Psalm 22. Then the
myth upon which Schreiber builds so much is at variance with Mark
on at least five points, as L. E. Keck has shown ("Mark 3:7-12 and
Mark's Christology," JBL 84 (1965), pp. 341-58, especially 355-6).
Finally, some of Schreiber's exegetical arguments are unconvincing,
as Kelber (Kingdom and Parousia, passim) has shown (e.g. the six
days of the passion narrative discussed in n. 32 above).

52. Mark, pp. 74-92, 151-206.

53. J. Schreiber, "Die Christologie des Markus," ZTK 58 (1961),
154-83, especially 171f.

54. Lightfoot, Gospel Message, p. 115.

55. Ibid., p. 116.

56. Evans, JTS N.S. 5 (1954), 12.

57. Boobyer, BJRL 35 (1952/53), 336, 338.

58. Evans, JTS N.S. 5 (1954), 12.

59. Cf. Gaston, No Stone, p. 483 n. 3.

60. The older literature is critically reviewed in H. J. Ebeling, Das
Messiasgeheimnis und die Botschaft des Marcus-Evangelisten (BZNW)
Berlin: A. Töpelmann, 1939. A more recent survey and discussion
of the problem is G. Minette de Tillesse, Le Secret messianique
dans L'Evangile de Marc (Lectio Divina) Paris: Les Editions du
Cerf, 1968.

61. Critics generally recognize that there is a strong element of

Markan redaction in this section of the gospel. See, e.g.,
Burkill, Mysterious Revelation, pp. 259 n. 3, 294 n. 19.

62. JBL 84 (1965), 348-51.

63. Tradition, p. 224 n. 2.

64. Auerbach, Mimesis (New York: Doubleday Anchor Books, 1957),
     pp. 35ff. Cf. W. A. Beardslee, Literary Criticism of the New
     Testament (Philadelphia: Fortress Press, 1970), pp. 22ff.

65. Amos N. Wilder, The Language of the Gospel. Early Christian
     Rhetoric (New York: Harper & Row, 1964), p. 38: "a kind of
     sacred drama or oratorio."

66. Quoted in N. Perrin, What is Redaction Criticism? p. 6.

67. G. Bornkamm, 'Der Auferstandene und der Irdische. Mt. 28, 18-20,'
     Zeit und Geschichte (Bultmann Festschrift), Tübingen: J.C.B. Mohr,
     1964, pp. 171-91. G. Strecker, 'The Concept of History in
     Matthew,' JAAR 35 (1967), 219-30.

68. Beardslee, Literary Criticism of the New Testament, pp. 18-21,
     especially 21.

69. Taylor, Mark, p. 9.

Norman Perrin on Methodology in the Interpretation of Mark:

A Critique of "The Christology of Mark" and "Toward an Interpretation of the Gospel of Mark" *

by Edward C. Hobbs

The work of Norman Perrin has been the occasion of increasing scholarly pleasure, astonishment, and irritation during the
past decade. Pleasure, at being able to enjoy the fruits of a
most remarkable scholar's remarkable research in the problem
areas of New Testament literature; astonishment, at seeing things
turned around for such a different look, or cast in such a different light, than that to which we were accustomed; irritation, at
having to re-work and re-think so many aspects of our work which
rested on what we thought were settled foundations. The "Son-of-
Man" researches by Perrin during the last few years have especially occasioned the latter two responses; the present two papers
under discussion especially occasion the first, most particularly
in this critic of them on this happy celebration of Perrin's work.

"The Christology of Mark: A Study in Methodology" is an effort to suggest a way out of the impasse redaction criticism has
met in the study of Mark hitherto (because we do not have direct
access to his sources, in contrast with the situation vis-a-vis
Matthew and Luke), the way out being the blending of three methods

---

*Two papers by Norman Perrin, presented to the New Testament
Colloquium for discussion at its meeting of 23 October 1970 in
New York. The present paper is a slightly revised version of the
critique prepared for that meeting. All comments are based on
the drafts of the two papers distributed to the Colloquium, of
course, and not on any later revisions for publication.

or lines of approach, which hopefully will converge in such a way
as to reveal the theology of Mark. The three methods Perrin suggests "blending" are redaction criticism itself (through study of
literary factors of vocabulary and style, through study of particular Markan concerns, through attention to Markan compositional
techniques, and through isolation of definite units of pre-Markan
tradition and observation of Mark's use of these units), a search
for the model or literary form Mark is creating or imitating, and
the use of the insights of general literary criticism. Perrin
then carries out a test, or probe, or sample investigation, to
demonstrate the possibilities inherent in this blend of approaches;
the matter he chooses to investigate is Mark's Christology. He
contends that each of these three avenues of approach must be explored, and must be held in tension with one another.

A brief consideration of key points in the gospel from each
of these three approaches leads him to the conclusion that "the
Christology of Mark may best be approached by assuming that he uses
'Christ' and 'Son of God' to establish rapport with his readers
and then deliberately reinterprets and gives conceptual content
to these titles by a use of 'Son of Man'." Further, the Son of
Man Christology prior to and in Mark is clarified: "Prior to Mark
there are three uses of Son of Man in the tradition: use in an
apocalyptic context, use in reflection upon the significance of
the ministry of Jesus, and use with (para)didonai in apologetic
for the Passion. From these beginnings Mark develops the threefold emphasis which is characteristic of his gospel--apocalyptic,

authority in the present, suffering . . . ." Thus these conclusions, though not new, validate the approach suggested by Perrin,
because they emerge from the combination of methods he suggests
combining, and similar attack on other aspects of Markan theology
and purpose is indicated as a next step.

"Towards an Interpretation of the Gospel of Mark" is somewhat
analogously concerned with methodology, not only in its final section (VIII), which bears the same title as the entire essay, and
focuses on five separate aspects of the hermeneutical task, but
also in the approach followed in the bulk of the paper, namely,
structural analysis. Perrin does this on the ground that Mark is
an author, and in some sense consciously shaped his work, creating
a new whole out of existing smaller units of tradition. Mark is
the first structured narrative gospel, and it is therefore appropriate to begin with structural analysis. By following this out,
he is led to the conclusion that Mark "is the last and greatest
representative of that dynamic impulse in earliest Christianity
to conceptualize one's own experience, understanding and circumstances in the form of sayings of the pre-Easter Jesus and of
stories of his ministry in Galilee and Judea." Previous instances
of this practice were the Christian prophets (apocalyptic Son of
Man sayings), Christian scribes (Jesus debating and teaching),
Christian communities (controversy stories), each of whom created
the Jesus tradition as the appropriate form in which to conceptualize their present experience and understanding. But Mark went
one step further: he put it together "in the form of a coherent

story with a beginning in Galilee, a middle in Caesarea Philippi
and a climax in Jerusalem." The consequence was remarkable:
"The nature of the material he was using and his purpose in using
it was such that the result was mimetic narrative and this fact
created a possibility that had not been there before: the possibility of involving his readers in the gospel story as a whole
rather than in some particular part of it, such as a controversy
story, the Lord's Supper paradosis, or even a connected passion
narrative."

The resulting possibility of this structural analysis and of
the mimetic-narrative character of the gospel as thus analyzed is
to show the purpose of the evangelist. It is "to catch the attention of his reader and lead him from Galilee through Caesarea
Philippi to Jerusalem and the empty tomb, and to the realization
that he, the reader, is being challenged to discipleship in the
context of the prospect of the coming of Jesus as Son of Man."
The two subsidiary or auxiliary purposes are the combatting of a
false Christology (held by the disciples in the narrative), and
the giving of the discipleship parenesis (the climax of each of
the three prediction units).

In the final section, Perrin suggests five "standpoints" from
which hermeneutics must be engaged in. They are: (1) the philosophy of language, embracing such names as Bultmann, Heidegger,
Gadamer, and "the new hermeneutic;" (2) historical criticism;
(3) literary criticism; (4) history of religion; and (5) history
of Christian hermeneutics. He argues that the second has made

great progress, the first presents great difficulties but must be done with respect to the next two, and the third is in its infancy. The fourth and fifth he adds as perhaps not having received sufficient attention. But his conclusion, scarcely argued for but only affirmed, is that the second (later called "the first" for some reason), historical criticism, has "normative influence," or should have it, and should exercise normative influence and control over the others.

But in fact, the striking feature of both papers is that Perrin has devoted himself heavily to a dimension of the third standpoint or method--literary criticism. The shape of his method is not so much to be found in his "structural analysis," for there he simply follows "generally accepted opinion" as to the "broad. . . geographical outline to the gospel." Rather, the distinctive methodological principle he formulates and follows is this: regardless of the origin of a particular saying or pericope or bit of redaction, the use to which the Evangelist puts it can be determined, and is of decisive importance in the interpretation of the document as a literary construct. "The origin of the saying is less important in our immediate context than the use to which Mark puts it . . .", and later, "Be that as it may [viz., the redactional history of the passion-predictions], the use of the predictions by Mark is not in dispute." This methodological principle is one whose use is in part vindicated by its results in the hands of Perrin, as he himself points out in the last sentence of the Christology paper; indeed, surely that is the main

point of the paper, as may be seen by doing very elementary literary criticism on the paper itself! The title carries as its
second phrase "A Study in Methodology;" the introduction, which
focuses on methodology, but especially on the place of literary
criticism in the "blend" since it has been unjustifiably neglected
by New Testament scholars, carries the matter forward; the fre-
quent use of "but regardless of the origin, or the oral-tradition
history, or redaction-history, of the item, we can observe Mark's
use of it in his literary construct," or words to that effect,
confirms the point; and his final paragraph clinches it.

It is difficult to do other than say that Perrin has amply
proved his point methodologically, by investigation of th s one
aspect of the Gospel, and that the vindication of the method deserves to be followed by extensive studies in the Gospels along
these lines. It affords me personally some satisfaction at seeing
the methodological principle vindicated (indeed, at seeing it
noticed!), inasmuch as fifteen years ago I published a plea that
the Gospels can and should now be studied as literary wholes, as
works standing in their own right with their own internal and integral organizing principles, which can be discerned and utilized
in the interpretation of the Gospels by means of the literary-
critical method.* Of course, many New Testament scholars will
protest that they have already in fact been doing just this sort

---

*Edward C. Hobbs, "A Different Approach to the Writing of
Commentaries on the Synoptic Gospels," in A Stubborn Faith:
Papers on Old Testament and Related Subjects Presented to Honor
William Andrew Irwin, edited by Edward C. Hobbs. Dallas: Southern
Methodist Univesity Press, 1956. Pp. 155-163.

of thing; but they have not, except haphazardly, generally in ig-
norance of what real literary critics do in their work. (The
glorious exception is obviously Amos Niven Wilder, a predecessor
of Perrin at Chicago.) Perrin has engaged in a process which deserves continuation and development, not only by himself, but by
the coming generation of New Testament scholars.

The most negative comment to be made about the two papers
is with respect to the question of discovering the appropriate
model or models in terms of which to see Mark's purpose(s). (This
is the "second line of approach" in the Christology paper.) Perrin
correctly points out that one model was the synoptic tradition
itself--this is of course a commonplace since the rise of form
criticism. But what is missing in both of these papers (and indeed is missing in almost all work on the Gospels, with minor
exceptions), is serious attention to a source of models very heavily mined by Mark and probably by all of the Evangelists. That
source is the Old Testament. I do not mean that Old Testament
citation and explicit reference in matters of terminology or titles
is avoided; but I mean models in the sense Perrin uses the term,
that is, structural models, or literary models. The success of
Perrin's own defense of the literary-critical method should
prompt a return to this source. In particular, I would hope that
the Exodus as a major model for the construction of the Gospel
would be reconsidered with some seriousness. In addition to major
overall questions it provides answers for, it often explicates
minor items better than alternatives do.

As an instance of a minor item being illuminated by the Old
Testament model theory, especially the Exodus model, we might
note the matter of "after six days," in Mark 9:2. Perrin says
that this "is of real significance for Mark;" he argues that its
point is "after three days, the resurrection; after six days, the
parousia" ("Interpretation," pp. 4, 12-14, 17). That is, Mark
stands with his readers in the second "waiting period," that between resurrection and parousia, the transfiguration being the
proleptic account of the parousia. I find this quite persuasive,
but incomplete, and without any model for the "after six days,"
unlike the "after three days," whose ultimate origin in the tradition is found in Hosea 6:2. Were the Exodus-model already being
considered as a major source-model for Mark, this detail would fall
into place quite simply as follows:

Exodus 24 follows the giving of the Law and the Holiness
Code; it says that Moses is to ascend the mountain, in the company
of Aaron, Nadab, and Abihu, plus 70 elders of Israel. They do
so, and the God of Israel is seen, with a pavement of sapphire
stone under his feet, like the very heaven for clarity. Then Moses
goes further alone, and the glory of the Lord, in the form of a
cloud, settles on the mountain for six days; after six days, i.e.,
on the seventh, the Lord speaks out of the cloud. After Moses
descends from the mountain, he finds that his followers have been
faithless (the Golden Calf has been made), and the Lord utters
angry words about their faithlessness, and decides he will bear
with them no longer. Moses' intercession, however, results in the
nation being spared.

That Moses ascends with three close companions, two of them brothers, may not seem too much of an echo of Jesus ascending the mountain with three close companions, two of them brothers; but when we add the facts that the revelation of the Lord occurs there, that God speaks out of the cloud, and it is <u>after six days</u>, succeeded by discovery of the faithlessness of the disciples when they descend, and complaining words about the faithless followers are heard from "the Lord," the case for this model as a clue, or this clue as a model, becomes strengthened. Dare I add that when Moses finally descends from the mountain (Ex. 34:29-25), "the skin of his face shone because he had been talking with God," so that he had to put a veil over his face when he spoke to the people?

Recognition of the pervasive character of this model, the Exodus, would be beneficial in many ways, I believe, not least of them the confirmation along other lines of the thesis put forward by Perrin (and others) that Mark points forward to a parousia-fulfillment as a major purpose of his work. But showing how this is so would require a major paper, for which there is neither time, space, nor occasion here.

Let me now turn to Perrin's solution to the Messianic Secret materials of the Gospel, and raise a question about it. It is certainly the case that it must be worked out in literary terms as well as in other ways; but <u>all</u> of the evidence must be taken into account, and this is just what very few commentators do. (Perrin is not alone in this, and my question goes to all such

explanations.) The Gospel is actually a remarkable <u>mixture</u> of
secrecy and openness about Jesus' role. Cf. 4:22--"There is nothing hid, except to be made manifest; nor is anything secret, except to come to light." This theme can be taken, and usually is,
to mean that the manifest character of Jesus' role comes only at
the end of the Gospel. But consider the following details (once
considered, as for example by Wrede, to be evidences of Mark's incomplete carrying out of his thesis):

Mark 1:11--a voice from heaven announces Jesus as the Son,
the Beloved, quoting Psa. 2:7 and Isa. 42:1 to do it.

Mark 1:24-28--The demoniac in the synagogue acclaims Jesus
as the Holy One of God; Jesus commands the demon to silence, not
to exclude the knowledge of his identity, but rather because the
command to "be muzzled" is used in gaining control over such powers
as demons and natural forces (it is the same verb in 4:39, where
the wind is addressed together with the sea). The outcome of
this pericope is that "his fame spread everywhere at once, throughout all the surrounding territory of Galilee." Hardly a secret!--
and there is no hint that Jesus is displeased. The general statement in 1:34 is simply an extension of the point that acknowledg-
ment by demons is not the testimony Jesus seeks, as well as an
affirmation of his power over them, shown by his "muzzling" them.

Mark 1:40-45--the leper, who is "cleansed" (the key word,
repeated by Mark three times, as "raise" is repeated three times
in the following pericope), is told not to speak to anyone. Here
is a command to secrecy; but in contrast, the <u>next</u> person to be

cleansed, the hemorrhaging woman (5:25-34), tries to keep it a
secret, yet is forced by Jesus to testify to the cleansing before
a "great crowd"! This suggests a different pattern, a pairing
of healings into secrecy-manifestation as the model; first a
cleansing to be kept secret, then a cleansing to be made manifest;
first a blind man to keep the healing a secret, then a blind man
to make it manifest; etc. But this is not the place to discuss
that hypothesis--I only mention it to suggest there is overlooked
evidence in the literary-critical field.

Mark 2:1-12--Jesus raises a man in public, with no command
to secrecy, so that "they were all amazed, and glorified God."
Yet the previous story of raising, Simon's mother-in-law, was not
done in public, but in a private home. (No command to secrecy,
however.)

Mark 5:1-20--the Legion-demoniac is told by Jesus to go and
proclaim among his friends how much "the Lord" had done for him;
he goes off and proclaims "how much Jesus had done for him; and
all men marvelled."

Mark 5:43--Jesus commands them to be silent about the resurrection of Jairus' daughter. (But in ch. 16, the women are ordered to "go, tell.") Resurrection #1, silence ordered; Resurrection #2, telling ordered.

Mark 7:32-37--a deaf-mute is healed, and commanded to silence.
But in 9:14-29, the next deaf-mute is healed only after Jesus
sees a crowd come running together--a public display, with no
silence requested or ordered.

Mark 8:22-26--the blind man of Bethsaida is healed, and told "Do not even enter the village;" or perhaps it is a command to silence, a variant that has enormous support in the textual tradition, though widely varying in form. (C. H. Turner argued for this latter reading, in JTS 26, p. 18.) But the other blind man healed, Bartimaeus (10:46-52), is only healed after a great hue and cry is developed, with much public attention. No silence is ordered.

All of this suggests something other than a "secrecy motif"--rather, there seems to be a hidden-then-manifest motif, a secret-later-made-known in pairs of healings. The healings involved seem to be the sorts expected when "that Day" arrived (e.g., Isa. 35:3-7). At the very least, there is not a simple "Messianic Secrecy" theme in Mark's materials!

Taken altogether, both of Perrin's articles very convincingly show how a literary-critical approach will confirm the hypothesis that Mark's attack on one or more popular Christologies of his time, which used the popular titles of "Christ" and "Son of God," is launched via his own development of the already-extant "Son of Man" tradition, a tradition which applied this title in the same three contexts Mark applies it. Mark's development of it along all three lines as a vehicle for attack on the theios aner type Christology already has been partially anticipated in redaction-critical ways; but Perrin vindicates the literary critical approach as leading to the same result, perhaps even more clearly. This is another dimension of the strength of Perrin's use of the

literary critical method for investigation of a theological problem in the Gospels.

In all, these two essays by Perrin mark out significant
directions for New Testament scholarship to follow in the coming
years; his great strength is in his actual vindication (by way
of a "Probe") of his methodology by means of concrete exegesis of
the text itself. It is altogether too easy to spin hermeneutical
theories in the armchair; Perrin has done better--he has tried
them out! More--with success!

Notes on a Pilgrimage:

Norman Perrin and New Testament Christology

by Victor Paul Furnish

In 1968 Norman Perrin wrote: ". . . a good deal of my academic pilgrimage in these past ten years might be described as a
coming to terms with [the opening sentence of Bultmann's Theology
of the New Testament],"[1] namely, that Jesus' message is a pre-
supposition of New Testament theology and not a constituent part
of it. Indeed, some of the steps in this academic pilgrimage
are visible as one surveys the articles and reviews published by
Perrin between 1959 and 1968, the themes of most of which converge
in the topic of New Testament christology. In order to identify
and summarize Perrin's chief concerns and principal contributions, it may be useful to discuss the content of these articles
under three headings: The Historical Jesus and the Gospel Traditions, the Origins and Development of Christology, and the Marcan
Christology.[2]

I.   The Historical Jesus and the Gospel Traditions

Perrin's interest in reopening a "quest for the historical
Jesus" was expressed in an article, written in collaboration
with William R. Farmer, which surveyed certain "post-Bultmannian"
developments in the work of Käsemann, Bornkamm and Fuchs. The
authors' intention was to show that Bultmann's own students were
becoming convinced that their teacher's sharp distinction between the historical Jesus and the Christ of the kerygma was
overdrawn. Special emphasis was placed here on Käsemann's increased confidence in what can be known about Jesus' authentic

teaching,[3] on Bornkamm's increased confidence in what can be known
about Jesus' work[4] and in Fuchs' apparent readiness to speak about
Jesus' own attitude.[5] Perrin and Farmer welcomed these developments and concluded that even scholars who espouse "radical New
Testament criticism" and center attention on the post-Easter kerygma
have found it possible to speak of the "theological significance
of the historical Jesus."[6] This "makes it imperative that theologians should direct their attention to the historical Jesus as
a legitimate object of Christian faith and as a first concern of
Christian theology."[7]

One could have anticipated, in view of this co-authored article and its principal conclusion, that Perrin's own subsequent
work would involve further attention to historically authentic
data about Jesus in the gospels and the significance of the historical Jesus for the church's faith. These interests continue to
be present, indeed, but instead of becoming increasingly confident
of what can be known about the historical Jesus (taking his place
in the Käsemann-Bornkamm-Fuchs continuum schematized in the 1959
article), Perrin seems to become increasingly less confident respecting knowledge of the historical Jesus. Or, put positively,
he begins to lay more stress on the theological intention of the
gospels through which the historical Jesus must be sought: "They
are a unique combination of historical report and kerygmatic
theology, the purpose of which is, however, through and through,
proclamation and not historical reporting."[8] While he still
agrees with Käsemann that the christology of the kerygma "is already

implicit in the teaching of Jesus,"[9] he will eventually come to
the point of wanting to disassociate himself from the line taken
earlier, that "there is _enough_ historical evidence in the New
Testament to demonstrate that Jesus acted and taught in such a
way" as to make Kasemann's point valid.[10] The new quest for the
historical Jesus initiated by Käsemann is _not_ a matter of increasing "the extent of our knowledge of that figure but of the significance of such knowledge, however limited it may be in extent."[11]

What, now, is Perrin himself prepared to say about the significance for faith of the historical Jesus? Whereas the earlier
Perrin-Farmer position had stressed the importance of the historical Jesus as "a legitimate object of Christian faith" and as
"a first concern of Christian theology,"[12] Perrin himself now
takes a markedly different stance: ". . . the nature and purpose
of the gospels as this is revealed by critical scholarship support Bultmann's understanding of the significance of the historical
Jesus for faith,"[13] which is (as Perrin describes it) that the
object of faith is the Christ of the kerygma, not the historical
Jesus. Moreover, Perrin now disclaims interest in "going back
to the concept of the historical Jesus as the central concern of
Christian faith. . . ."[14] Although, at the same time, he warns
about resting content with a "kerygmatic Christ" divorced from
the historical Jesus because this, like the first alternative,
would not "do justice to the early Christian identification of
earthly Jesus and risen Lord,"[15] he apparently does not find
Bultmann's view incompatible with his own.

The increasingly Bultmannian orientation of Perrin's "pilgrimage" is most evident in his 1968 article on "Recent Trends"
in the study of christology. Here he not only emphasizes that the
burden of proof lies "very heavily" upon those who claim that a
christological saying is authentic,[16] but he also shifts away
somewhat from his earlier stress (following Käsemann) on an implicit christology in Jesus' teaching: ". . . the starting point
for New Testament Christology is not the message of the historical
Jesus--not even the implicit Christology of that message--but the
theologizing of early Christianity."[17] More precisely, Perrin
believes that recent research shows christology to have been less
"a product of reflection upon the past event of Jesus" than a
product of reflection "upon the present 'experience' of Christians."[18]
How Perrin has reached this position is best seen in yet another
series of articles produced during these same years.

II. The Origins and Development of Christology.

Perrin has found the key to the origins and development of
christology in the "Son of man" sayings of the synoptic traditions.
His examination of these has led him to the conclusion "that there
can be no apocalyptic Son of man saying in the teaching of Jesus,"
and that all such synoptic sayings are products of the post-Easter
Christian community.[19] In this conclusion he agrees with Vielhauer,
Conzelmann and others. Perrin, however, has arrived at this conclusion in a distinctive way. He holds, contrary to most interpreters, that there simply was no unified "Son of man" concept in
Judaism, but instead "a variety of uses" of the imagery in Jewish

apocalyptic and the midrashic traditions.[20]   While the reference
to the Son of man in Dan. 7.13 (where a concept from Canaanite
mythology is used) is subsequently taken up in both I Enoch and
IV Ezra, there are major differences in the way it is employed.
In the earliest cycle of traditions in I Enoch (chapters 70-71)
Dan. 7.13 is used to help interpret the translation of Enoch; Enoch
becomes the Son of man.[21]   In the later Similitudes (I Enoch 46ff.)
Enoch is portrayed as the Son of man who reveals heavenly things
and who sits on a heavenly throne as the eschatological judge.   He
is now becoming a "pre-existent" figure in the apocalyptic sense,
and is even identified with the Messiah (48.10).[22]   In IV Ezra 13,
on the other hand, the vision of the man from the sea is an apocalyptic midrash on Psa. Sol. 17 and only slight use is made of Dan. 7.
Perrin argues that there are no significant relationships between
the traditions in I Enoch and IV Ezra.   In IV Ezra the man from the
sea is an apocalyptic redeemer figure who enjoys a kind of pre-
existence, but these are common features of all apocalyptic and
are inadequate to establish the identity of IV Ezra's "Man" and I
Enoch's "Son of man."[23]   Rather than a common Son of man conception
in Judaism, "we have . . . the imagery of Dan. 7.13 being used
freely and creatively by subsequent seers and scribes.   These uses
are independent of one another."[24]   (Subsequently, Perrin is able
to find confirmation of this in G. Vermes' contention that "Son
of man" was not in use as a title in Aramaic.[25])

    Perrin extends this conclusion to include the scribes of the
Christian tradition.   Working independently they use Dan. 7.13 as

one scriptural basis for the interpretation of Jesus' resurrection.
"Just as Enoch became Son of man on the basis of an interpretation
of his translation, so Jesus became Son of man on the basis of
an interpretation of his resurrection."[26] Three Christian exegetical traditions using Dan. 7.13 are identified. In one there
is emphasis upon Jesus' exaltation to God's right hand as the Son
of man (Acts 7.55f., using also Psa. 110.1). In a second Zech.
12.10ff. is also employed, now to help interpret the Messiah's
crucifixion; thus the exegesis has an apologetic purpose (Jn. 19.37;
Rev. 1.7). Finally, there is the apocalyptic use of Dan. 7.13
(Mk. 13.26 par.; 14.62 par.) which, however, is also somewhat related to the first two.[27] Perrin believes that the conclusion to
be drawn from all this is that "Christology begins with the interpretation of the resurrection as Jesus' exaltation to the right
hand of God as Son of man, i.e., with an interpretation of Christian experience in the light of Old Testament texts, rather than
with the identification of Jesus as Son of man in dominical sayings preserved in the tradition."[28]

Perrin expands upon and somewhat refines his view of the
Christian exegetical tradition by utilizing B. Lindars' conception of a Christian pesher type use of the Old Testament. This
occurred, he insists, as the church sought to understand and interpret "events within its own experience and aspects of its own
expectation. . . ."[29] As an instance of this he takes the saying
at Mk. 14.62 which he believes to be an interweaving of two
separate strands in the Christian pesher tradition. It is suggested

that one of these originated in an interpretation of the resurrection and used Psa. 110.1 and Dan. 7.13 (What elsewhere he referred to as one of three exegetical traditions in the church).
The other originated in an interpretation of the crucifixion and
used Zech. 12.10ff., expanded by a parousia expectation and further use of Dan. 7.13 (what elsewhere he referred to as the second
and third types of Christian exegetical tradition).[30] He believes
that the catalyst for the conflation of these two strands was their
common use of Dan. 7.13, "and the resultant combined pesher was
then historicized by being read back on to the lips of Jesus in
the tradition."[31] Mk. 14.62 thus typifies the process by which
christology originated and developed: first there was an "experience" or "expectation;" second, this was interpreted on the basis
of an Old Testament text (a Christian pesher); third, the material
was historicized by being formed into a narrative about Jesus or
being ascribed to his own teaching; and fourth, the pesher itself
or its historicization became in its turn the basis for yet further
theologizing.[32]

In one of his most recent articles Perrin has carried his
own investigations further and has, at the same time, been per-
suaded by some of the work of two others, S. Schulz and W. Kramer.
Thus, his sketch of the origins and development of christology
has become rather more elaborate. For his own part, Perrin has
expanded his study of the Son of man sayings. He notes that if
any of these are Jesus' own they would be the apocalyptic promises,
eschatological judgment pronouncements, eschatological correlatives

and exhortations to watchfulness. But he finds that the form of
the eschatological promise preceded any use of the Son of man
motif with it,[33] that reference to the Son of man "is neither
original nor extensive" in the judgment pronouncements,[34] that
the "correlatives" form (in Q) which is directly interested in
the coming Son of man was, however, "created specifically to give
content to a previously existing expectation,"[35] and that the
reference to the Son of man in Lk. 12.40=Mt. 24.44 has been added
to a previously existing exhortation to watchfulness (cf. Mk.
13.35f.; I Thess. 5.3f.; II Pet. 3.10; Rev. 3.3; 16.15).[36] Therefore, he claims, the New Testament itself can yield no such "formal category" as "apocalyptic Son of man sayings," from which
genuinely dominical Son of man sayings are usually sought.[37]

Perrin's view of the beginnings of christology is now also
extended by his employment of the results of the work of Schulz
and Kramer, to which he had not referred in earlier books or
articles. In agreement with them he now emphasizes the initial
importance of Psa. 110.1 for the formulation of a _mar_-christology
which included an expectation of Jesus' future coming again as
judge (Acts 2.32; Mk. 12.36; Heb. 10.12).[38] Here we have, then,
a _pre_-Son of man christology in the church, although from this
beginning, with the aid of Zech. 12.10ff. and Dan. 7.13, there
subsequently emerges the idea of Jesus as the apocalyptic Son
of man. This new element in his view of course does not alter
his major contention, which is that christology developed in
relation to the Christian exegesis of Old Testament texts and not
in relation to Son of man sayings in Jesus' own teaching.

Perrin's sketch of the development of christology is also
aided by his analysis of the Son of man sayings with a present
reference and those which speak of his suffering.[39] From this
analysis two additional features of the process emerge. One of
these is the role of Q which seems to have a special interest in
the Son of man concept. Q, he believes, "was formed under the
impetus of the expectation of the coming of Jesus as Son of man,
and it built up its collection of teachings of Jesus or teachings
by prophets in the name of Jesus as a body of material which men
could learn and follow in preparation for that coming."[40] In Q
"the tradition reflects upon the ministry of Jesus as the ministry
of the one who was Son of man designate, the ministry of the one
who was identical with the Son of man, and hence begins to modify
certain sayings which were products of that ministry or which
now can be fitted into it, or to produce sayings which embody
this reflection."[41] The characteristic form of this reflection
in Q is the "eschatalogical correlative," the correlation of a
past or present event with the coming Son of man (e.g. Lk. 11.30;
17.24 par.; 17.26 par.; 17.28, 30).[42] In Q, therefore, we are
in touch with a stage in the development of christology later
than that represented in the exegetical (Christian pesher) tradition.[43]

Perrin's further study of the Son of man passages has yielded
another added ingredient for his overall view of the development
of christology--the place and importance of the evangelist "Mark."
This evangelist, he now avers, "is the major figure in the

creative use of Son of man traditions in the New Testament period."[44] This aspect of Perrin's work deserves consideration in its own right.

III. The Marcan Christology

According to Perrin's view, a major part of Mark's purpose is christological: "to teach the Christians of his day a true Christology in place of the false Christology which he felt they were in danger of accepting."[45] In formulating this true christology (which the evangelist has read back into the ministry and teaching of Jesus[46]) Mark has employed various traditions available to him. First, there were the apocalyptic Son of man sayings as developed in the Christian pesher tradition[47]; these he can fit quite directly into the theological patterns of his gospel.[48] Second, he is heir to the tendency, observable in Q, "to reflect upon the ministry of Jesus as the ministry of the Son of man designate and eventually of the Son of man himself."[49] Mk. 2.10, 28, which stress Jesus' authority on earth, and Mk. 10.45, an I-saying about service which presents a soteriological interpretation of Jesus' death, are representative of this aspect of Mark's heritage.[50] Third, he unites two traditions which had used the concept of deliverance to interpret Jesus' passion.[51] Here Perrin depends on the work of H.E. Todt and F. Hahn who have isolated two types of paradidōmi tradition, a Palestinian type which sought to come to terms with Jesus' death and explain it to Jews and a Hellenistic type in which the soteriological

significance of the cross and its meaning for faith was developed.[52]
From these two traditions Mark formulated the passion predictions
and the teaching about discipleship.[53]

Perrin's identification of the pre-Marcan traditions used by
the evangelist does not lead him to minimize the Marcan contribution, however. On the contrary, he regards the christology of
Mark as a momentous, creative achievement. This evangelist has
integrated the various traditions into a coherent Son of man
christology which he then uses to give content to his contention
that Jesus is the true Son of God[54] (the two titles are juxta-
posed throughout the gospel[55]). Mark's own christology is specifically present between 2.10 and 10.45 where there is "a carefully arranged sequence of references"[56] to the authority[57] and
the suffering of the Son of man. The pattern this evangelist has
worked out moves us from the earthly authority of the Son of man
(2.10, 28), to his suffering (8.31), to his final authority in
judgment (8.38) and then to an extended development of the meaning
of suffering (chapters 9-10).[58] The climax comes in 10.45 which
also serves to introduce the passion story; here "we are in fact
at the heart of the Marcan theological enterprise."[59]

In summary, Perrin believes that Mark appropriated the Son
of man concept "because it was comparatively unused in the tradition before him and was not a confessional title," and because
he could unite within it all the points he regarded as most vital
about the Son of God: his earthly and apocalyptic authority, the
necessity of his suffering and the soteriological significance of

his death.[60] Finally, then, it is Perrin's judgment that in Mark
we have "not only the most creative moment in the use of Son of man
man in the New Testament," but "also one of the most creative moments in the development of the theology of the New Testament
altogether."[61]

Conclusion

A critical assessment of Perrin's thesis respecting the origins and development of christology lies beyond the scope of
this brief essay. The objective here has been, rather, to summarize his work on this topic as that is available in articles
and reviews, and to draw together its various facets in such a
way as to accentuate the most notable fruits of his labor. By
way of conclusion, then, I venture to identify three of these and
subsequently to offer some reflections upon the whole course of
the "pilgrimage" these articles reveal.

To begin with, it is readily apparent that Perrin has effectively challenged the common notion that the origins of New
Testament christology lie in the church's use of apocalyptic Son
of man sayings which were found already on the lips of Jesus.
Perrin's challenge has been two-pronged. First, he has demonstrated the difficulty--indeed, he himself would say the impossi-
bility--of locating within Judaism one unified conception of a
transcendent, sovereign, apocalyptic Son of man. This conclusion is of basic importance for everything else he does, and the
evidence adduced to support it, as well as the evidence normally
marshalled to support the contrary conclusion, needs to be

re-examined in the light of Perrin's work. Moreover, he himself
has suggested that this conclusion regarding "Son of man" might
also be appropriate with respect to "Messiah," "Son of God" and
"Son of David." Were any of these, he asks, designations for
"hard and fast conceptions in Palestinian and hellenistic Judaism,
respectively, in the period under consideration"? Was it not
difficult to maintain such "titular distinctions" in New Testament times?[62] The other prong of Perrin's challenge fastens on
the synoptic sayings themselves as he questions whether even here
there is any formally identifiable category of apocalyptic Son
of man sayings.

This brings us to a second major contribution from Perrin--
his proposal that the roots of christology lie exclusively in
the church's exegesis of the Old Testament, in the Christian
pesher traditions. Here, to be sure, he has utilized the work of
other scholars, but he has at the same time sought to show in
some detail how particular Old Testament texts were appropriated
and integrated in the formulation of a Son of man christology.
Perrin suggests that here, too, his work might be extended to
cover other titles--perhaps to "seek a pesher-type use of II
Samuel 7 (and related texts) in early Christianity as the basis
for the formulation of a Son of God Christology."[63]

In the third place must be mentioned Perrin's work on Mark.
He finds in Mark's achievement the most creative and decisive
moment in the development of New Testament christology, and the
verve and insight with which he has approached the analysis of

Mark's theological project suggests that he himself is convinced his most important contributions can be made here. If his initial conclusions about Mark's purpose, methods and christology are sustained, one may expect considerable new light to be shed not only on the theology of this evangelist, but also on other theological currents and eddies within the broad stream of earliest Christianity.

Finally, then, what are we to say about this ten year pilgrimage which began with the first sentence of Bultmann's Theology of the New Testament? Has Perrin "come to terms" with that sentence, and if so, in what way? I have already indicated that Perrin now seems much closer to Bultmann's position than when he began his pilgrimage. As his work has proceeded he has shown less interest in identifying within the church's preaching a concern for the specifically "historical Jesus," and increasingly more interest in the church's response to the resurrected Christ. In reading the articles reviewed here one is impressed with the number of times Perrin refers to the church "reflecting" on its own present "experience." Thus, in commenting on Fuller's book-- which he calls "a milestone in the study of the beginnings of Christology . . ."[64]--Perrin suggests "that we should emphasize even more than Fuller does the fact that Christology is a product of Christian experience and the possibility that the synoptic tradition is a product of Christian reflection."[65] In another place Perrin identifies several aspects of the "present experience" of Christians which prompted reflection and produced christology.

Among these were: their consciousness of being an eschatological community, their confrontation with Judaism and the attendant
apologetic needs, their facing a delay of the parousia and their
dispersion into the Gentile world.[66] But his list is headed, and
elsewhere he mentions almost exclusively, the importance of Jesus'
resurrection. From the context of his work it is clear that he
is not thinking of the resurrection as an event of the past to
which the earliest Christians looked back. Indeed, he specifically says that christology was "not so much" produced from reflection on "the past event of Jesus" as from "the present 'experience' of Christians."[67] It is then, within the post-Easter
community that christology has its roots, within a community
that sought to understand the meaning of the resurrection and of
its own existence according to biblical, namely, Old Testament,
texts.

From all this it would seem easy to conclude that Bultmann's
position respecting the relation of Jesus' message to New Testament theology has been embraced by Perrin. He is now certainly
very close to it. But at the same time he is concerned lest it
be forgotten that the earliest Christians identified their risen
Lord "absolutely and completely" with the earthly Jesus;[68] for
this reason he believes that the message of the historical Jesus
requires attention. In his latest work Perrin does not pursue
this point, however, and he gives us only the slightest hint of
the line he might wish to follow out, namely, the relationship
between Jesus' preaching of the coming kingdom of God and the

church's later identification of Jesus himself with the coming
Son of man.[69] But if the question which prompted this pilgrimage
is no longer Perrin's major interest, that in no way diminishes
the character of his academic trek as a true pilgrimage. It is
no aimless peregrination. His articles reveal it to be a thought-
ful, disciplined, purposeful exploration of some of the most
fundamental and sensitive issues of Christian theology.

FOOTNOTES

1. "Recent Trends in Research in the Christology of the New
    Testament," in Transitions in Biblical Scholarship ("Essays
    in Divinity," Vol. VI), ed. J. Coert Rylaarsdam (Chicago and
    London: The University of Chicago Press, 1968), p. 231.
    (Hereinafter cited as "Recent Trends.")

2. Perrin's two books published in the decade under considera-
    tion (The Kingdom of God in the Teaching of Jesus, 1963 and
    Rediscovering the Teaching of Jesus, 1967) fall outside the
    limited scope of this present paper, although especially the
    second of these two gathers together and presents in more de-
    tail some work published first in articles. The following
    articles and reviews do come in for consideration here: "The
    Kerygmatic Theology and the Question of the Historical Jesus"
    (with William R. Farmer), Religion in Life, XXIX, 1959-60, pp.
    86-97 [cited as "Historical Jesus"]; "The Challenge of New
    Testament Theology Today," Criterion, IV, 1965, pp. 25-34
    [cited as "New Testament Theology"]; "The Son of Man in An-
    cient Judaism and Primitive Christianity: A Suggestion,"
    Biblical Research, XI, 1966, pp. 17-28 [cited as "A Suggestion"
    "Mark xiv. 62: The End Product of a Christian Pesher Tradi-
    tion?" New Testament Studies, XII, 1966, pp. 150-155 [cited
    as "Mark xiv. 62"]; "The Wredestrasse Becomes the Hauptstrasse:
    Reflections on the Reprinting of the Dodd Festschrift," The
    Journal of Religion, XLVI, 1966, pp. 296-300 [cited as "Wrede-
    strasse"]; "New Beginnings in Christology: A Review Article"

[of R. H. Fuller, <u>The Foundations of New Testament Christology</u>], <u>The Journal of Religion</u>, XLVI, 1966, pp. 318-19 [cited as "New Beginnings"]; "The Son of Man in the Synoptic Tradition," <u>Biblical Research</u>, XIII, 1968, 3-25 [cited as "Synoptic Tradition"]; "The Creative Use of the Son of Man Traditions by Mark," <u>Union Seminary Quarterly Review</u>, XXIII, 1968, pp. 357-65 [cited as "Mark"]; and the article cited in n. 1.

3. "Historical Jesus," pp. 89-91.

4. <u>Ibid</u>., pp. 91-94.

5. <u>Ibid</u>., pp. 94-95.

6. <u>Ibid</u>., p. 96.

7. <u>Ibid</u>., p. 97, italics added.

8. "New Testament Theology," p. 27.

9. <u>Ibid</u>., p. 30.

10. "Historical Jesus," p. 91, italics added.

11. "Wredestrasse," p. 299; although in "New Testament Theology" published a year earlier he had still spoken of knowing "enough" about Jesus' teaching to be able to agree with Käsemann (above, n. 9).

12. "Historical Jesus," p. 97.

13. "New Testament Theology," p. 20, italics added.

14. "Wredestrasse," p. 300

15. <u>Ibid</u>.

16. "Recent Trends," p. 221

17. <u>Ibid</u>., p. 231.

18. <u>Ibid</u>., p. 223.

19. "A Suggestion," p. 27; "Recent Trends," pp. 221, 232.

20. "A Suggestion," p. 20. Perrin's argument is later incorpor-
    ated into his book, Rediscovering the Teaching of Jesus,
    especially pp. 164-99.

21. Ibid., p. 21f.

22. Ibid., p. 22f.

23. Ibid., p. 24f.

24. Ibid., p. 26.

25. Perrin cites Vermes' article, "The use of Bar Nash/Bar Nasha
    in Jewish Aramaic" published as an Appendix in the third
    edition of Matthew Black's An Aramaic Approach to the Gospels
    and Acts ("Synoptic Tradition," p. 5, n. 6).

26. Ibid., cf. "Synoptic Tradition," p. 5, n. 7.

27. "A Suggestion," p. 26f.

28. Ibid., p. 28; cf. "New Beginnings," p. 495.

29. "Mark xiv. 62," p. 150.

30. Ibid., pp. 151-54.

31. Ibid., p. 155.

32. Ibid., p. 150.

33. "Synoptic Tradition," p. 7f.

34. Ibid., p. 8.

35. Ibid., p. 10.

36. Ibid.

37. Ibid.

38. Ibid., p. 4.

39. *Ibid*., pp. 11-20. The only one of these sayings he traces
    back to Jesus (cf. Rediscovering the Teaching of Jesus, pp.
    119-21) is that of Lk. 7.34 par. But here, he argues, "Son
    of man" is not a title, but a self-designation in accord with
    the common Aramaic idiom--although in Q it is given a chris-
    tological meaning ("Synoptic Tradition," p. 14).

40. *Ibid*., p. 14.

41. *Ibid*., p. 15.

42. *Ibid*., p. 10. Perrin here acknowledges the work of his stu-
    dent, R. A. Edwards.

43. See Perrin's summary of the stages, *ibid*., p. 11.

44. *Ibid*., p. 20.

45. *Ibid*., p. 21.

46. Perrin also accepts the view that the disciples in Mark are
    representatives of an errant christology (*ibid*.).

47. *Ibid*., p. 21.

48. "Mark," p. 364.

49. "Synoptic Tradition," p. 21.

50. *Ibid*., p. 24f.; "Mark," p. 365.

51. "Synoptic Tradition," p. 21f.

52. *Ibid*., p. 18f.

53. *Ibid*., p. 18; "Mark," p. 365. Perrin also acknowledges other
    elements forged into the passion predictions, notably (follow-
    ing Lindars) the use of Psa. 118 in the Christian exegetical
    tradition ("Synoptic Tradition," p. 20).

54. "Synoptic Tradition," pp. 21, 23; "Mark," p. 365.

55. "Mark," p. 358.

56. "Synoptic Tradition," p. 23.

57. Perrin stresses this theme in Mark and emphasizes that "_exousia_ is never used of the earthly Jesus in the synoptic tradition except in Mark or in dependence on Mark" (_ibid_., p. 18). Cf. "Mark," p. 361.

58. "Synoptic Tradition," pp. 22-24.

59. _Ibid_., p. 24.

60. _Ibid_., p. 24f.; cf. "Mark," p. 365, where Perrin also mentions Mark's concern to show that "the necessity for suffering is laid also upon the disciples. . . ."

61. "Mark," p. 365.

62. "New Beginnings," p. 496.

63. "Recent Trends," p. 225.

64. "New Beginnings," p. 496.

65. _Ibid_., p. 495.

66. "Recent Trends," p. 223.

67. _Ibid_.; see also p. 232.

68. "Wredestrasse," p. 300.

69. See "Synoptic Tradition," p. 14, where it is suggested that Q's "link with the teaching of the historical Jesus is possible because Jesus himself had proclaimed the coming of the kingdom of God."

<u>Norman Perrin on the Kingdom of God</u>

An Appreciation and an Assessment from the Perspective of 1970

by Eldon Jay Epp

It is no coincidence that within a year's time three similar
books appeared in English, two of them carrying not only the
same date, but the same title:

> Gösta Lundström, <u>The Kingdom of God in the Teaching of Jesus</u>.
> Edinburg: Oliver and Boyd, 1963.

> Norman Perrin, <u>The Kingdom of God in the Teaching of Jesus</u>.
> Philadelphia: Westminster Press, 1963.

> George Eldon Ladd, <u>Jesus and the Kingdom</u>. New York: Harper
> & Row, 1964.

The time was ripe for these works, particularly for the extensive
historical surveys contained in the volumes by Lundström and
Perrin. The reason is simple enough: Amos N. Wilder's master-
fully concise summary of Jewish and New Testament eschatology in
his 1950 revision of <u>Eschatology and Ethics in the Teaching of
Jesus</u>[1] had served well to trace out for the English-speaking
world the lines of the emerging concensus that the Kingdom of
God--in the teaching of Jesus--had both a present and a future
aspect. [Regrettably, Wilder's work was overlooked by Lundström.]
By the 1960's, however, a larger scale assessment was called
for; after all, post-war New Testament scholarship was only beginning to re-establish its cosmopolitan character and its in-
ternational communication in the early 1950's, as attested for
example by the first appearance of <u>New Testament Studies</u> in 1954
and <u>Novum Testamentum</u> in 1956, or by noting (in the present context of the study of the Kingdom) the increase of references to
English-language works in the second edition of W. G. Kümmel's

<u>Verheissung und Erfüllung</u> which appeared in 1953 and which, in
this respect, was exceptional for a German work of the time. It
was precisely this period from the end of World War II until the
middle 1950's which spawned such studies as those by Kümmel (1945),
Oscar Cullman (1946),[2] and Joachim Jeremias (1947),[3] as well as
those by the pupils of Rudolf Bultmann,[4] all of which reflected
and were the embodiment of this consensus on the Kingdom of God,
though variously interpreted to be sure. By the early 1960's
the time had come to place into perspective this now long-standing
discussion of the Kingdom of God in the gospels and to move on
from there. The three works mentioned at the outset sprang up
almost at once, each prepared independently of the others and
each attempting to fill the void with an integrating study.

This is not the place to compare and contrast these three
books which appeared in 1963-64; the works of Lundström and Perrin,
for example, were treated in a single review written, most appropriately, by Amos Wilder,[5] and Ladd's work was subjected, in the
same journal, to the biting criticism of Norman Perrin.[6] It is
clear, however, that of the three, it is Perrin's book which
stands out not only as the most useful but as the one which carries
forward the discussion; hence, with the perspective of seven years,
it remains the one to consult and will continue to serve students
and scholars in this way for some time to come. Praise from
one's opponent is hard-earned and doubtless to be esteemed more
highly than praise from one's friends; if so, George Ladd's words
are both appropriate and significant here: "Perrin has given

us a thoroughly competent, well-written, stimulating book, which
is strongly to be recommended as a history of interpretation of
this theme."[7] Not only is it a well-ordered and lucid volume,
but a skillfully concise one, consisting of only 215 pages (compared with 314 and 382 pages for Lundstrom and Ladd, respectively)
and yet providing both a more careful summary and a more detailed
critical evaluation of various views on the Kingdom from Ritschl
and Weiss on through to the pupils of Bultmann than normally expected or possible in a work of this size. This is not to say
that there is perfect balance throughout the volume; certainly
Rudolf Otto deserves more space than a single--though panoramic--
footnote to the discussion of C. H. Dodd, plus two other references, both of which indicate, by the way, influences of Otto upon
scholars figuring largely in Perrin's survey, namely T. W. Manson
and Bultmann.[8] Along the same line, the insufficiency of the
chapter on "The American View of Jesus as a Prophet"[9] has been
underscored suitably by American reviewers and notably by Amos
Wilder, himself one of those whose views are misdeemed in the
chapter.[10]

To stay with the debit column a moment longer, there may be
some justification--at least on the face of it--for George Ladd's
allegation that "Perrin's conclusions are based more on inter-
action with the history of criticism than with exegetical data,"[11]
but it is precisely in this connection that our 1970 perspective
on Perrin's book leads to a noteworthy observation (though one
which will be obvious to all who know his subsequent writings):[12]

In The Kingdon of God in the Teaching of Jesus the presentation
of detailed exegesis is, in fact, limited, though by no means
absent; it appears particularly in the final chapter when Perrin
presents his own position as it arises out of the survey and
criticism of the earlier scholarship. It would seem appropriate,
therefore, to describe the full range of Perrin's writings, like
the Kingdom itself, as possessing "present and future" aspects
in terms of "fulfillment and promise" (if one may utilize these
established phrases in their temporal meaning without prejudice
thereby to Perrin's own views of the Kingdom), for in a very
real sense The Kingdom of God in the Teaching of Jesus represented
a "present fulfillment" in 1963, which carried within itself the
"promise" of a "future consummation." The new fulfillment of the
promise emerged in 1967 as Rediscovering the Teaching of Jesus.[13]
It is equally clear to the reader of this second work, however,
that it too must be described a "fulfillment and promise;" the
book as a whole enlarges upon and, by extended and meticulous exegesis, settles much of that which was sketched late in the first
work, and yet the second volume--again predominantly the final
chapters which treat inter alia the apocalyptic Son of Man sayings and knowledge of the historical Jesus--brims with promise.
In fact, the "Preface" to Rediscovering the Teaching of Jesus contains the very word when Perrin says that his solution to the
apocalyptic Son of Man sayings appears "to offer promise as an
avenue of approach to the whole problem of the formation of
christological traditions in the early Church,"[14] and then

specifies this as his next sphere of concern. Papers published
or written subsequently do indeed show that the fulfillment is
"in process of realization."[15]   It should be possible to apply
this "promise-fulfillment" motif also to the relation between
Perrin's two major works and the two very recent smaller works
from his pen, The Promise of Bultmann [title coincidental!] and
What is Redaction Criticism?[16]   Although these last two volumes
are not so explicitly autobiographical as The Kingdom of God in
the Teaching of Jesus and Rediscovering the Teaching of Jesus,
clear lines of development can be traced through the stages represented within the first two until their full development is
reached in the second two volumes in their respective subjects,
namely existentialist interpretation and the form-criticism/
redaction-criticism complex. To give a more specific instance
with respect to the latter subject, Perrin's writings document
for us some of the stages in his transition from a basic source-
critical methodology (à la one of his two teachers, T. W. Manson)
to an unqualified form critical approach. In The Kingdom of God
in the Teaching of Jesus, while criticizing Manson's interpretation of the Kingdom, Perrin offers his own judgment that "there
is a steadily increasing recognition of the role of the early
Church in the shaping and combining of the material in the Synoptic Gospels."[17]   That such a statement originated in the 1960's
rather than the 1930's may have surprised most of us, but the
striking "conversion narrative" only four years later in Rediscovering the Teaching of Jesus[18] is as convincing and as satisfying

as the earlier statement is surprising. The outworking of his newfound form critical methodology is evident, of course, in the pages which follow that account, as well as in his further articles and his small book on redaction criticism--that second stage of form criticism.

An obvious conclusion from all of this is that Norman Perrin's "view" is not to be discerned from a random or indiscriminate reading of his earlier writings, but all his work must be re-checked against later stages in his discussion of a given subject. Both the rapid progression in his development and his "openness for the future" in scholarship constitute a challenge and an inspiration to every working scholar.

We have pressed sufficiently the analogy between the present and future aspects of the Kingdom of God and Norman Perrin's cre-atively unfolding studies which move from promise to fulfillment; we need not carry this further--we need only to hope in the pro-mise and await its fulfillment.

FOOTNOTES

1. New York: Harper, 1950, pp. 9-70. (The first edition, 1939, pp. 3-54, which covered generally the same ground, was thoroughly updated for the 1950 revision.)

2. Christus und die Zeit (Aurich, 1946); English trans. Christ and Time (Philadelphia: Westminster, 1950; Revised edition with a new introductory chapter, 1962).

3. Die Gleichnisse Jesu (Zürich, 1947); English trans. The Parables of Jesus (London: SCM, 1954; Revised edition, New York: Scribners, 1963).

4. See the references in Perrin, The Kingdom of God in the Teaching of Jesus, pp. 120-129.

5. Interpretation 18 (1964): 199-204. Other early joint reviews were by V. C. Pogue in Scottish Journal of Theology 17 (1964): 103ff.; W. E. Hull in Review and Expositor 61 (1964): 87ff.; E. Esking in Theologische Zeitschrift 20 (1964): 440-1; and A. M. Denis in Tijdschrift voor Theologie 5 (1965): 210ff.

6. Interpretation 19 (1965): 228-231. See Ladd's response in his The Pattern of New Testament Truth (Grand Rapids: Eerdmans, 1968), pp. 57-63; cf. pp. 47 n.12, 48.

When Perrin characterizes Ladd as taking his stand "squarely in the midstream of the contemporary concern about eschatology--with his face turned resolutely upstream, whence we all came some considerable time ago" (p. 231), the statement undoubtedly is justified. Yet it is important to see George Ladd's work in its own proper context, for his study of the

"Kingdom of God" began many years before his 1964 publication and arose out of a soul-searching struggle with the notion of the Kingdom in that branch of American (and British) fundamentalism known as "Dispensationalism" (see Ladd's Crucial Questions about the Kingdom of God [Grand Rapids: Eerdmans, 1952]). His views of the Kingdom, hammered out in this conflict, were derived by interacting critically with the classical and standard works on the subject: Weiss, Dalman, Schweitzer, Otto, Dodd, and the like, and the result was a position which sharply removed him from his own "Dispensational" heritage. Indeed, seen within its own context, George Ladd's change of views on the Kingdom of God was as decisive and crucial for him as was Norman Perrin's "conversion" to form criticism [discussed below].

Finally, while Ladd himself may be facing resolutely upstream, at the same time he has taught a number of his students, including the present writer, those skills which make it possible to navigate the mainstream of modern critical scholarship.

7. Ladd, The Pattern of New Testament Truth, p. 47 n.12.

8. Perrin, The Kingdom of God in the Teaching of Jesus, p. 59 n.4; pp. 172, 113.

9. Ibid., pp. 148-157.

10. See Wilder, Interpretation 18 (1964): 202-3; cf. also B. H. Throckmorton, Journal of Biblical Literature 83 (1964): 80.

11. Ladd, The Pattern of New Testament Truth, p. 58.

12. Ladd did not have this perspective in 1966 when he presented the lectures which comprise the work just cited, though he does have one reference (p. 59 n.37) to Perrin's Rediscovering the Teaching of Jesus, which was added, obviously, while preparing the lectures for publication.

13. New York: Harper & Row, 1967.

14. Perrin, Rediscovering the Teaching of Jesus, p. 12.

15. See Perrin, "The Creative Use of the Son of Man Traditions by Mark," Union Seminary Quarterly Review 23 (1967/68): 357-65; idem, "The Son of Man in the Synoptic Tradition," Biblical Research 13 (1968): 3-25; idem, "Recent Trends in Research in the Christology of the New Testament" (ed. J. Coert Rylaarsdam. Chicago: University of Chicago, 1968), pp. 217-233; idem, "The Christology of Mark: A Study in Methodology," a paper for the annual meeting of Studiorum Novi Testamenti Societas (August, 1970) [as yet unpublished]; and to some extent his recent paper at the New Testament Colloquium (New York, 1970): "Towards an Interpretation of the Gospel of Mark," [unpublished].

The phrase, "in process of realization," as all will recognize, is Ernst Haenchen's and was accepted by C. H. Dodd as describing accurately his own view [The Interpretation of the Fourth Gospel (Cambridge, 1953), p. 447 n.1], after it was reported by J. Jeremias [see The Parables of Jesus (English trans., London: SCM, 1954), p. 159 n.2; (Revised edition, 1963), p. 230 n.3].

16. <u>The Promise of Bultmann</u> (Philadelphia: Lippincott, 1969), in
the series "The Promise of Theology," edited by Martin E.
Marty; and <u>What is Redaction Criticism</u>? (Philadelphia: Fortress Press, 1969), in the series "Guides to Biblical Scholarship," edited (New Testament Series) by Dan O. Via, Jr.

17. <u>Kingdom of God in the Teaching of Jesus,</u> p. 96.

18. <u>Rediscovering the Teaching of Jesus</u>, pp. 11-32; cf. 52-3, and
Perrin, "Recent Trends in Research in the Christology of
the New Testament" (ed. J. Coert Rylaarsdam. Chicago: University of Chicago, 1968), pp. 227; 230-1. W. G. Kümmel's review of <u>Rediscovering the Teaching of Jesus</u> came to hand
after the present paper had been completed, but it is worth
adding that Perrin's "conversion" (as we have called it) to
form criticism was so thoroughgoing that Kümmel feels compelled
to close his review by calling Perrin "a radical representative of form critical and at the same time existentialist
Jesus research" [<u>Journal of Religion</u> 49 (1969): 66].

The Historical Jesus:

Some Comments and Thoughts on Norman Perrin's
Rediscovering the Teaching of Jesus

by Helmut Koester

Norman Perrin's book Rediscovering the Teaching of Jesus is
a masterpiece. The form critical method is consistently applied
for a convincing reconstruction of the history of individual units
of the synoptic tradition. The eschatological preaching of Jesus
which is thus rediscovered emerges in its own peculiarity; it no
longer appears as a composite construct that is derived from
general references to various eschatological concepts of the period. It is a historical Jesus--not a modernized Jesus--who is
nevertheless clearly distinguished from his environment and from
subsequent Christian developments.

A detailed critical discussion of the book would only be
able to question a few minor points. It would not be able to
alter significantly any of Perrin's conclusions. Therefore, I
want to use this opportunity to reflect about some basic problems
which came to my mind while rereading the book. I trust that
this is the most fruitful way to continue this discussion.

I should add that the following questions are not specifically directed to Norman Perrin. His book exhibits in an exem-
plary fashion certain presuppositions which all of us share who
have learned from Bultmann. Thus, it is a critique of my own
assumptions and perspectives as much as it wants to challenge my
friend Norman Perrin to reassess what we think can now be taken
for granted.

The main problem is that of the central criterion for the reconstruction of historical Jesus materials: the criterion of "dissimilarity." No doubt, this criterion functions very well and it is difficult to imagine how any critical analysis could proceed without it. It has been used successfully in previous attempts (Bultmann, Bornkamm) and Perrin's accomplishment is largely to be attributed to its consistent application. Indeed, only this criterion can prevent the illegitimate transfer of related, "similar" phenomena from the religious environment into the teaching of Jesus.

There is, however, one consideration which limits the usefulness of this criterion: the emphasis upon that which is dissimilar prevents a perspective in which the developmental processes come into view. "Dissimilarity" is always observed within the development of a particular stream of tradition. The continuous flow of such streams often does not even become discontinuous by the occurance of "dissimilar" phenomena within it.

To emphasize the criterion of dissimilarity may indeed tell us what were the peculiar features of Jesus' teaching. But it does not always guide us in our search for the relationship of Jesus' teaching to his Jewish tradition and environment, nor does it necessarily lead us into the problems of nascent Christianity in its quest to establish and confirm a continuity of its own beliefs with Jesus and his teachings or works.

This limitation of the principle is, e.g., visible in the whole problem of messianic titles or, more general, of the

expectation of the coming of any particular messianic figure.
Norman Perrin's conclusion that Jesus neither used any messianic
title for himself nor referred to any future messianic figure
should not be questioned. There are sufficient primitive traditions in the Synoptic Gospels, "dissimilar" from both, contemporary Jewish and later Christian, messianic beliefs, which strongly
support this conclusion. This, however, does not yet clarify the
relationship of Jesus' eschatological preaching to his immediate
background and context. Is it to be understood as a conscious
and deliberate break with a tradition that was dominated by the
expectation of one or several future messianic figures? Such
expectations are found in Qumran as well as in a number of Jewish
apocalyptic writings. But can we presuppose that this was indeed the background over against which Jesus' own eschatological
proclamation is to be evaluated?

It is by no means impossible that Jesus was not at all concerned with such beliefs and expectations as are expressed in
Qumran or in (later!) written Jewish apocalypses (even if he knew
any of the materials which we now possess--but even that assumption must remain questionable). Jesus did not write his proclamation, nor did he request his disciples to preserve in writing
what he had said. The romantic explanation that Jesus and the
most primitive Christian tradition belonged to a stage of cultural
consciousness that had not yet discovered the possibilities of
written communication, is not very appealing, even though it is
secretly and unwittingly held by many scholars. The explanation

that the coming of the kingdom of God in the imminent future made
writing a superfluous luxury, is, perhaps, a little more appropriate; but it does not get to the heart of the matter.   In
view of the fact that even in antiquity writing could be used as
a means to make communication more urgent and more effective (cf.
e.g., the prophet Jeremiah), the only appropriate reason for
Jesus' proclamation being oral would be that this was a peculiar
concomitant of the form and content of his message.   In this
respect, Jesus' message is "dissimilar" from the message of apocalyptic prophets who wrote "Revelations."   But we have not yet
discovered Jesus' dissimilarity from other prophets whose messages
required a "similar" oral communication.

   It has become an accepted dogma among New Testament scholars
to disregard the parallels to Jesus' ministry which are preserved in Josephus' reports about messianic prophets of the first
half of the first century A.D.: Judas the Galilaean (Ant. 18.23f=
Judas the Gaulanite or Galilaean of Ant. 18.44ff; Bell. 2.118?),
Theudas (Ant. 20.97f), the Egyptian prophet (Ant. 20.169f; Bell.
2.261), John the baptist (Ant. 18.116ff), and others.   Several
of these were called prophets, but there is no hint in Josephus'
reports that anyone of them proclaimed the coming of a future
messianic figure.   On the contrary, about Judas the Galilaean and
his followers Josephus says explicitly that "they accepted God
alone as their leader and master" (Ant. 18.23).   Other characteristics of such messianic prophets and their movements, as reported by Josephus, connect certain features of primitive portions

of the Synoptic tradition even more closely with these Palestinian prophets: the working of miracles and signs (e.g., Ant. 20.168),
the wilderness motif (Ant. 20.167, etc.), and the gathering of
people on the Mount of Olives (Ant. 20.169), cf. also the eschatological rite of baptism (Ant. 18.117). Synoptic materials which
exhibit "similarities" with these features of eschatological prophetic movements should not, on this basis, be excluded in the
attempt to rediscover the teachings of Jesus. On the contrary,
these similarities could be used in order to establish the appropriate context to which the eschatological prophecy of Jesus belongs. What is peculiar to Jesus' teaching must be argued within
this particular context, rather than in comparison with the expectations of messianic figures in Jewish apocalyptic literature.

As a result, the emphases--not necessarily the general out-
lines of the picture of Jesus' teaching--would be different.
Jesus' proclamation of the imminent coming of the kingdom of God
would no longer appear as an unusual feature in his message, since
it seems that this feature is similar to the proclamation of
Theudas, the Egyptian prophet, John the baptist, and others--but
it is most likely historical, in spite of this similarity. On
the other hand, even greater emphasis would have to be placed
upon that which now emerges as peculiar to Jesus' teaching within
this general frame of comparison. Let me draw special attention
to one of these elements: the wisdom teaching of Jesus. This
would refer to a large portion of very primitive sayings materials in the Synoptic Gospels (it is commonplace that many sayings

of Jesus belong to various forms of wisdom sayings), but also to
many so-called eschatological injunctions as preserved in Mt. 5
which are in fact wisdom sayings.

The Testimonium Flavianum (Josephus Ant. 18.63)--if genuine--
could be a remarkable witness to this peculiar feature of Jesus'
ministry: Jesus is called a "sophos," i.e., a wise man, and a
teacher. To be sure the present form of the Testimonium Flavianum
most likely results from Christian tampering with the original
Josephus text. But the unusual characterization of Jesus as a
"wise man" may very well be a remnant of Josephus' original characterization of Jesus. If this is the case, it is noteworthy
that Josephus does not use this term for any other messianic prophet of this period. That Josephus could have preserved a characterization of Jesus' ministry which has been suppressed by the
mainstream of the Christian tradition, is not at all impossible.
With respect to John the baptist, Josephus says that he did not
preach baptism as a means to gain pardon for previous sins, but
as a seal of the body for those whose souls were already right-
eous (Ant. 18.117). This conflicts with the view of the canonical Gospels which present John as a preacher of the baptism for
the remission of sins (Mk. 1:4f par.)--most probably a second
transfer of a widely held early Christian understanding of baptism to John the baptist.

Thus, on the basis of Josephus' reports one would expect to
find that Jesus belonged to those "messianic" disturbances with
which the Romans had to deal during this period, but that he was

distinguished as a "wise man" (I will omit, for the purposes of
this paper, the equally intriguing reference to Jesus' signs and
miracles).

This suggestion, it would seem to me, implies some questions
with respect to another shortcoming of the principle of "dissimilarity." Norman Perrin follows Bultmann in the exclusion of
many synoptic wisdom sayings from the original teachings of Jesus.
To be sure, wisdom sayings are notoriously elusive with respect
to questions of authorship and date. Just about all of the wisdom sayings in the Synoptic Gospels--not only the famous Golden
Rule--seem to have so many parallels in the Jewish, Christian,
and pagan tradition, that we are accustomed to accept the conclusion that not a single one of these sayings can be argued to be
characteristic of Jesus' original proclamation. The criterion
of dissimilarity, therefore, eliminates the wisdom sayings of
the Sermon on the Mount: Mt. 5.13f; 5.29f; 6.19f,21,24, 25-34;
7.1-2, 3-5, 6; but also such sayings as Mk. 4.21-25; Mt. 10.28ff;
Lk. 12.47f; 14.7-14 and many others. But also several wisdom
parables are not considered, such as Lk. 12.16ff. Other parables
of this type, e.g., Lk. 14.28ff and Mt. 13.44-45f, 47f are only
treated since they can be interpreted to exhibit some eschatological features, and Mk. 2.21f--a wisdom saying in every respect--
is included, since it can be understood as an "eschatological
simile." In the Gospel of Thomas the same saying is clearly a
wisdom saying. Why is it unlikely that the tradition of Jesus
as a teacher of wisdom in the Gospel of Thomas is a direct

continuation of the teaching of the historical Jesus? Why do we
require from a wisdom saying that it must have an eschatological
twist in order to qualify as an original saying of Jesus?

I am not suggesting a whole-sale acceptance of the wisdom
materials as part of the teaching of the "historical Jesus." But
these materials constitute a considerable portion of the synoptic sayings tradition. What is their origin? Do we have to look
for special eschatological applications of these materials in
order to be able to assign them to Jesus' teaching? If wisdom
sayings which exhibit no peculiar eschatological features do not
originate with Jesus himself--who introduced them into the tradition of his saying? (This is not a rhetorical question.) Among
the prophetic sayings of the Gospel of Thomas a comparatively
large number are synoptic sayings which Bultmann (and also Norman
Perrin) assigns to the historical Jesus. But few, if any, of
the wisdom sayings of the Gospel of Thomas would even be considered
candidates for this distinction. It is certainly correct that
we have not yet developed any criteria which would enable us to
write a history of the tradition of wisdom sayings. Thus, it
remains difficult for us to trace the trajectory of those sayings from the Jewish wisdom movement through their use in Jesus'
teaching to the early church and to the beginnings of gnosticism.
James Robinson, in his LOGOI SOPHON, has demonstrated that this
trajectory existed. But he has done it primarily through an
investigation of quotation formulae and general references to
these sayings. What still remains to be done, is the tracing

of the history of these sayings themselves and of their forms
and contents.

The critical analysis of the eschatological sayings of Jesus
which began with Bultmann has found a good conclusion in Norman
Perrin's book. Eschatological sayings which predict the coming
of a "messianic" figure, or which speak about a distance between
present and future, cannot be assigned to the historical Jesus.
On the other hand, Jesus' eschatological teaching is expressed
in sayings which speak about the miraculous presence of the Kingdom, i.e., primarily in the parables. This amazingly clear and
unambiguous picture of Jesus' teaching has great appeal. Nevertheless, the relationship of the tradition of wisdom sayings to
the historical Jesus remains an open question. It can be safely
predicted that a solution of this question will alter the rediscovered teaching of Jesus and will make it more complex and less
unambiguous--provided that the question of the wisdom sayings
and of their trajectory is solved on its own terms and is not
forced into the rediscovered schema of Jesus' eschatological
teaching.

With respect to the eschatological preaching of Jesus there
is an underlying reason that might justify the criterion of dissimilarity: the early Christian kerygma proclaimed Jesus as
risen and as coming again. By contrast, Jesus in his eschatological message did not proclaim himself nor any future messianic
figure. Thus kerygmatic and historical materials would have to
be radically dissimilar. With respect to the wisdom sayings as

well as the miracles it is not possible to assume such a radical
break. If Jesus was a teacher of wisdom, so did his disciples
continue to teach this wisdom. If Jesus performed miracles,
his apostles continued the enactment of such powerful deeds. There
is no obvious problem of continuity with the historical Jesus
in either one of these relationships to him. Consequently, the
criterion of dissimilarity may not at all be applicable to the
analysis of the pertinent materials. I would like to suggest
that one must search for characteristic shifts within the historical processes which characterize the tradition, its trans-
mission and its applications. Can any such characteristic shift
be attributed to the historical Jesus? Perhaps that is not possible or not very likely insofar as the wisdom tradition is concerned. But that should not necessarily eliminate Jesus from
the process of tradition which leads from Judaism to Christianity.
Thus it may be that we are left with a rather ambiguous result
as long as we focus our interest upon the problem of the peculiarity (not to say: the uniqueness) of Jesus.

On the other hand, the historicity of Jesus and of his
teaching is radicalized. It is quite possible that "historical
Jesus" implies that in many, perhaps in all, respects Jesus is
just one link in a chain, one step in a development of various
religious trajectories. In this respect, the historian does not
have to accept the burden of the systematic theologian who is
no longer willing or able to formulate the uniqueness of Jesus
in terms of a mythological or metaphysical presuppositions.

The historian's answer may well be that Jesus was not only not unique, but that it is also very unlikely that Jesus' life and ministry was peculiar and clearly distinguishable from other "similar" religious movements, traditions, and persons of his time.

Norman Perrin, in the last chapter of his book, speaks about the distinction between the tasks of the historian and of the theologian. He points to the "vicissitudes of historical factuality" which would seem to threaten the theologian's judgments. Ultimately the problem is resolved by a separation of the functions. The historian's insight and the theologian's presuppositions are two different things, even though knowledge gained from historical investigation is permitted to challenge the believer's view "in any age."

I wonder whether this solution has really taken account not only of the vicissitudes, but also of the embarrassment of historical factuality. "Vicissitudes" can be understood to include the fact that the results of historical investigation may change from time to time, and that historians are sometimes wrong. But I would like to speak of embarrassment, because the results of historical scholarship are always and by their very nature controversial, no matter how relatively certain they may be in any particular instance. Furthermore, the historian can never be sure in advance whether the result of his study will be something that is unique or peculiar or spectacular. On the contrary, the more remarkable and spectacular the result, the more suspicious the historian must be with respect to his own methods and procedures.

It is not unlikely that the historian has to despair of the task to provide the kind of inspiring and useful insight into the historical Jesus which theologians (and ministers and people interested in religion and some well-meaning revolutionaries) would welcome. Of course, theologians have often felt that historical scholarship is a rather unreliable handmaiden and, therefore, have sometimes preferred to rely upon the more tangible evidence of archeology which has thus become a useful substitute for history. But all this must not lead the historian to secure and fortify selfishly his own realm of freedom and to allow the theologian and the believer to be challenged occasionally by the results of historical scholarship whenever it happens to be opportune, worthwhile, and edifying.

Christianity is belief in Jesus. Therefore, Christian faith cannot exist without facing the embarrassment of the historical Jesus. Religious revelation and edification is normally gained from the fact that the source of such edification transcends and surpasses ordinary historical experience. This is the case also in such religious orientations which draw their primary inspiration from history, be it the history of a nation which thus must be glorified in its origins and destiny and purified in its course (as it is told in school books), or be it the history of a religious community which is usually remembered

and taught in stories of saints and superhuman success (pace
ordinary people and events, not to speak of evildoers and fail-
ures).

The historian has not only the right, but also the duty to
protest, and he must make this protest heard outside of the walls
of his academic community. If the historian happens to deal
with the origins of the Christian community and with Jesus--I
do not care whether or not he thinks that he is a Christian--his
task is an eminently theological one. If theologians and church-
men or reformers and revolutionaries think that history is only
useful for propaganda purposes in order to enhance and culti-
vate the religious establishment or in order to overthrow it and
substitute a new one, then the historian may be the only one who
can still speak as a theologian, i.e. speak in behalf of the
truth.

Truth requires that the believer must face the embarrass-
ments of history as they are exposed by historical scholarship.
In terms of traditional Christian doctrine this is a question of
the doctrine of incarnation. It is dangerous to understand the
particularity of historical phenomena to include of necessity
such elements as "peculiar," "dissimilar," "unusual," and "out-
standing." Particularity means first of all that which is a
specific moment's actual experience insofar as it cannot be
fitted into general concepts of philosophical, religious, or
rational values. Jesus' life, ministry, teaching, and death was
probably not peculiar and unusual, but it was particular as the

experience of one specific human being. In some respects, this
particular human life can be distinguished from other men's
lives; in other respects, however, this will not be possible,
because distinctions did in fact not exist. But these latter
realities and contingencies of Jesus' life are therefore no less
"historical," and they are no less relevant theologically. In
fact, they constitute the humanity of Jesus in a more fundamental
way than any of the peculiar or special features--in the words
of Paul: "born by a woman, born under the law."

On this basis one could go one step further in the question
of the relationship between the historian's and the theologian's
task. Not only is the exposure to the "vicissitudes of historical factuality" an eminently theological task, but for the historian who investigates the tradition about Jesus and its trans-
mission, there is another theological enterprise connected with
his scholarly task: to investigate the vicissitudes of a faith
which remains bound to the embarrassment of a "historical" revelation and to a tradition which preserves this historical fact
as a challenge to faith in any new age. To separate the historian's and the theologian's task in this enterprise will im-
poverish the historian and it will increase for the theologian
the danger of speculating about assumed truths and values instead of thinking about people in their particular historical
experiences.

Norman Perrin, <u>What is Redaction Criticism?</u>

by Amos Wilder

Guides to Biblical Scholarship, New Testament Series, Philadelphia: Fortress Press, 1969.

This book like the series to which it belongs reports on
biblical critical method and achievement of a period now in many
ways drawing to a close. Since the book is not only an admirable
exposition of its topic but one in which the continuing problems
emerge, it will not only be useful to the uninitiated but invites
reflection here on the future agenda especially of the study of
the Gospels.

The series includes other volumes, one dealing with literary
criticism and the other with form criticism. The editor of the
series in his Foreword recognizes the inter-relation of the
three. Moreover, he observes that in the case of literary criticism new approaches to "the philosophy of language," and to the
relation of literary structures to meaning and existence, are
being recognized. This has not been so evident in form criticism
and in redaction criticism as practised, and our present author,
understandably, does not enter this area. But it is here that
we shall wish to make some observations.

The main body of the book offers a beautifully clear and
vigorous account of the origin and flowering of the discipline
in question. Professor Perrin begins with the demise of the Marcan hypothesis and shows how the work of Wrede in this connection set the stage for form criticism, which in its turn, by
necessity, directed attention in this new light to the Gospels
as wholes. The ground greaking studies of the Synoptic Gospels

by Bornkamm, Conzelmann, and Marxsen, as well as by R. H. Lightfoot in England, are examined with perceptive detail. A useful
sample of the procedure is provided, and the book closes with
discussion of the significance of the discipline and its relation
to such matters as biblical theology, the historical Jesus and
the Gospel form itself.

In this relatively brief introduction to the topic the author
largely identifes himself with the categories in which form criticism and redaction criticism have been pursued. But there is
good reason to think that these categories and assumptions are
being questioned today. This applies not only to biblical criticism but to general literary and historical criticism as a whole.
It is a question of the best perspective for appropriating ancient writings. It may be that the tools and focus of observation associated with modern literary method have not been fully
suited to what these writings have to say. In any case, Norman
Perrin's review of one branch of such study suggests some of
these questions just because he is so faithful to the authors
whose procedure he is describing.

I begin with a matter that may seem incidental, but I present it as an example of the discomfort I feel with the now recognized schema which Perrin follows. This schema he identifies
with the royal road which leads from the "Wrede-Strasse" through
form criticism to the "Haupt-Strasse" of redaction criticism.
This is certainly one essential approach. But it bothers me
that it does not seem to account for the work, for example, of

my old teacher Benjamin W. Bacon. His early and important work on the stages of the tradition, and on the final work of the evangelists, Matthew and John, in their own right and situation—and in primary relation to patristic and proto-Gnostic contexts—all this took shape for him apart from acquaintance with the form critical pioneers. The point of this observation is not to disparage the form critics but to suggest that our understanding of the Gospels in their composition as wholes may well be served by other strategies. Indeed, any too rigorous linking of redactional criticism with form criticism may even handicap the task. In this connection too I would point to a continuing obscurity about the relation of redaction criticism to genre criticism, a matter to which I shall return.

In the second place I find some confirmation of this hesitation when I turn to a book like Lars Hartman's _Prophecy Interpreted_ (1966). Hartman's study of the "midrashic" and paraenetic shaping of apocalyptic material in the Jewish and early Christian tradition shows that this material is not always amenable to form critical control, especially so far as these critics think in terms of _Kleinliteratur_ (see pp. 210-211; 251-252). The "school" activity on the tradition associated with the names of Riesenfeld, Stendahl and Hartman is not easily accommodated to form critical and redaction critical operation. If we look at Mark 13 and its parallels in their terms, for example, the shaping of the tradition as well as the version espoused by the particular evangelist in redaction take on new meaning. No

doubt life-situation layers are still discernible and are related to the transformations in question. But more justice can
be done to the subtle process of historization of the Old Testament models as well as to the free play with the transmitted
mythos.

But this is connected with a more significant level of observation. In the work of certain Scandinavian scholars (though
one may well discount an excessive preoccupation with the historicity of the tradition) one often finds a more adequate sense
of the dynamics of the apocalyptic language--perhaps related to
their special initiation in religious phenomenology and liturgical
interest. The form critic thinks of the morphology of a passage
and its life-situation in somewhat objective terms, and this
stance carries over into redaction study. Thus J. Rohde stresses
the fact that form criticism and redaction criticism agree in
their primary interest in the literary aspect of the writing of
the Gospels. Questions of Sache are dealt with therefore in
quasi-external ways, and are referred to as the "theology" of the
author. Hartman, on the other hand, is concerned with the vital-
ity of the transmitted Old Testament eschatological passages and
their subsequent "midrashic" modifications. Such texts, he observes, are "active" and not "passive" (p. 139) and thus are not
at the disposal of the ultimate evangelist in the way that a formal unit would be.

But by this path we reach a wider observation. As we have
suggested, the shaping, arranging, composing activity of the author

of a Gospel has its final criterion in his "theology." We find
a recurrent distinction between the "history" and the "theology."
The redactorial operations are dictated by "theological motiva-
tion." The "theology" of the evangelist may be broken down into
ecclesiology, Christology, eschatology, etc. But we should face
the fact that these categories have a quasi-rationalist character. Here form criticism and redaction criticism betray the
subject-object approach to their material that belongs to the
whole history of scientific method.

In the field of secular literary criticism there has of late
been a reaction against the formal emphasis of the "new criticism"
for precisely this reason. Literary appreciation and interpretation in this approach treat the poem or play as object at
their disposal, even if it is to be delighted in. Two separate
schools of existential criticism here demur. On the one hand
that represented by the humanist hermeneutic of language represented by H. G. Gadamer. On the other that represented by the
"critics of consciousness" in France and Switzerland. The latter,
for example, are interested in the literary work as action not
object. They find the true reality of the work in the personal
myth of the author, whatever the materials he uses.

In his closing section Perrin goes deeper and invokes the
category of "experience," Christian experience, "experience of
the risen Lord" in which past experience and therefore "historicity" is grounded as well as future guarantees. This is also
one of the categories of the older historiography. Perrin is

wrestling with the problem of continuity between the historical
Jesus and the present encounter with him actualized in the tradition and in the final stage represented by the work of the
evangelist. But as with the category "theology" so with the
category "experience" the full reality of a writing and its coming to be is not brought to light.

Another example of those now questionable categories of
criticism is the way in which mythological images are understood.

> The ancient documents were written by people with a
> view of the world very different from our own. To the
> men of the New Testament, for example, the appearance
> of angels, the machinations of demons, the breaking
> open of the heavens to facilitate the descent of a
> dove or the ascent of a body are all events within the
> realm of realistic expectation, whereas the appearance
> of such things to us would send us to consult either
> an oculist or a psychologist! (p. 72)

But this misrepresents ancient mentality. It is anachronistic
to assign such an objective character to their expressions. Here
again we come upon the rationalist frame of mind in which criticism in the modern period has been carried out.

I have thus cited several points at which queries arise for
me with regard to the present schema of redaction criticism as
Perrin reports it. To summarize one can say that our inherited
categories of critical method--however great a contribution they
have made in the modern period--now stand in the way of a full
encounter with our writings, and even with the processes of their
coming to be. As James M. Robinson has noted (in the Introduction to a forthcoming volume), "The absence of an unmediated encounter with the original text was the initial source of

distortion in the categories adopted by modern critical scholarship." There is a disparity between the presuppositions of our
investigation and method, on the one hand, and the presuppositions behind the writing of the Gospels. It is a question of what
historical reality is. It is a question as to the ontology of
language. In the biblical material it is a question as to the
Sache. It would seem that form criticism and redaction criticism have not fully faced these questions.

How this dilemma is reflected in that final stage represented
by redaction criticism is worth exploring. Though our present
attempts to read a Gospel, as it stands, as the work of an author
and not of a mere compiler, frees us from earlier misunderstand-
ings, there still may be carry-overs associated with the history
of criticism which still color and handicap the undertaking.

Among the motifs of criticism which may today arouse our
suspicion is the genetic preoccupation of all historical study.
The prominence of this concern in connection with humanistic
study in the past is understandable: we see here the attempt to
dissipate error associate with a cumulative tradition or to trace
ideas or images to their root. But this historicist habit of
mind may still operate unconsciously to handicap a free encounter
with a writing in its final form. This question may, indeed,
be raised with regard even to such invaluable examples of redaction criticism as those of Marxsen, Conzelmann and Bornkamm.

Where would such handicaps and consequent distortions appear?
No doubt, for example, where excessive concern for "historical"

dating and placing of a Gospel intrude on an "unmediated encounter"
with it. Thus one could suspect that Marxsen's interest in iden-
itfying the occasion of the writing of Mark--i.e., with the re-
moval of the church from Jerusalem to Galilee at the beginning of
the Jewish War--may reflect a historicist preoccupation which
would otherwise limit his grasp of the work as literary whole.
The great merit of Paul Minear's recent study of the Book of Revelation, matters of detail apart, is that we are enabled to re-
spond to the language without unwarranted distraction by excessive
absorption in historical correspondences.

Similarly, a concern with the evolution of early Christianity
inherited from an older focus of critical scholarship--again
with genetic and historicist presuppositions--might stand in the
way of an immediate encounter with a Gospel and the intention of
its author. Here the work of Conzelmann might raise questions,
since he carries it out with a vivid awareness of the debate over
Frühchristentum. This is not to say that within that context the
work of "Luke" cannot be illuminated. It is, however, to ask
whether the older preoccupation with analyzing continuity and
change in terms of milieu--all in somewhat rationalistic and objective strategies--may not militate against a full appropriate
encouter with the writing.

The above considerations may seem highly abstract and far
removed from the exhaustive analysis of detail which must necessarily enter into any study of the composition of a Gospel or
any other writing. What we are in search of, however, is some

new key in which all such study can be done, and one in which
the limited horizon of the older methodology can be overcome.
The risks of such an attempt can be illustrated by Austin Farrer's
work on the Gospel of Mark. Paralleling contemporary literary
critical approaches to Shakespeare's plays and other secular writings, Farrer sought to identify the unity and structure of Mark
with symbolic motifs corresponding with image-patterns in the
Old Testament. In this way he sought to disclose the unity and
meaning of the Gospel at a more dynamic level. At one level, however, scholars disagreed with particular historical-critical
judgments incident to the larger undertaking. But at another
level a secular critic, Helen Gardner, argued that here as in
similar studies of Elizabethan texts an inadequate grasp of the
writing resulted. To locate the meaning of a work in such an
image-pattern was not only to lift it out of its rich life-setting
into a kind of Platonic ideality, but to ignore such essential
aspects as style in which the personal impress of the author is
felt. Thus the basic intention of the work can be obscured.

An unclarified area in the discussion of redaction criticism
is that of its relation to genre criticism. It is not enough to
redefine the task as "composition criticism" Even here our eye
is upon the author's role in selection, omission, alteration,
shaping, weighting of his material. In this sense our eye is
upon the author and his motives, but in a particular focus. The
intention of the author, fully understood, demands more.

The work of the author, finally, is determined by the genre he adopts. But here we must say two things. (1) The term "genre" ordinarily has such connotations that it may be better to use a less formal designation and say "medium." (2) The evangelist's adoption of a medium need not be thought of as a deliberate and conscious choice. What is to be retained here is the relation of his work to some kind of "public" expectation, and in this sense, literary convention. (This whole area is interestingly discussed by Norman R. Petersen in a paper prepared for the 1970 meeting of the Society of Biblical Literature: "So-Called Gnostic Type Gospels and the Question of the Genre 'Gospel'.") This is not a question of aesthetic form but of fundamental hermeneutic communication. In this sense the genre or medium of the work is of primordial importance and its meaning subtends all other aspects of meaning in the writing in question. Redaction criticism unless specifically pointing beyond itself to genre criticism should be so understood as to include this final stage where authorial intention and genre commitment meet. Even in the case of the Gospel of Mark, supposing it to be the oldest of our canonical Gospels and in that sense a novum, even here redaction criticism should come to terms with that dimension of meaning identified with the medium or shape of the writing in its relation to the rhetorical expectations of its readers at the time.

The Promise of Bultmann

by James M. Robinson

This volume of 1969 is part of the series The Promise of
Theology edited by Martin E. Marty, introducing a number of
modern theologians in a non-technical way in paperback format.
It is published at Philadelphi and New York by J. B. Lippincott
Company.

This is a remarkably lucid, accurate, and comprehensive presentation of the theology of Rudolf Bultmann. Indeed there is
probably no treatment of this intricate topic that in each respect
succeeds so well within such a limited format. One could not
wish for a better introduction to Bultmann to put in the hands of
a person who wants an overview that will not only provide initial
orientation but in retrospect prove to have anticipated guidance
sought at a much more advanced level.

Upon a brief analysis of Bultmann's life and times there
follows a series of topically ordered chapters, in terms of
Bultmann's academic rootage in existential philosophy and in
historiography, in the current theological alternatives of Jesus
and the kerygma, and in Bultmann's program for updating the
Christian message and the resultant promise of his theology for
the future. This well-organized presentation is completed with
brief notes and a selected annotated bibliography.

Lucidity of presentation--a must in such a series, yet a
well-nigh impossibility in dealing with such a topic--is achieved
to an astounding degree, indeed to such a degree that not only
are the pedagogical requirements of the series fully met, but
formulations are achieved which break new ground simply by the
force of thought presupposed in attaining them. To give an

illustration from the area of terminology: On p. 37 a dilemma
for every translator is accurately stated: "There are actually
four different conceptions (sc. of history) that need to be
taken into account. Unfortunately it is not possible to list
them entirely in English because the English language does not
have enough nouns to cover them. German does, but only because
the German language happens to have two different words for 'history' and the theologians decided, quite arbitrarily, to give
these words different meanings. The list then has to read: history as Historie; history as Geschichte. . . ." Indeed Historie
and Geschichte have entered the English-language theological vocabulary as loan words precisely because no translator could
adequately render them. At one time I considered using two variant English spellings and resultant meanings from the same Greek
etymology, "history" and "story," but abandoned this effort,
since "story" has become too unhistorical in overtone to do justice to Geschichte. Yet, a few pages later (p. 42), with the
nonchalance of seemingly effortless ease, Perrin produces the
best solution yet: "So as a historian, Bultmann is very much interested in Historie, the historical, but as an existentialist,
only in Geschichte, the historic." The adjective forms have for
some time been recognized as adequate translations, but no one
had thought of using them as the missing substantives!

     One of the major impediments in appropriating Bultmannian
theology and the related Heideggerian philosophy has been the intricate terminology and resultant barbaric English, which

inevitably attracted attention away from the issue and onto itself. Sticking within the confines of the official terminology
is for any writer the easy way out, since then it is the reader,
not the writer, who is held responsible for the paucity of ideas
resultant upon working through the terminological undergrowth.
Indeed such a painful procedure might even be preferable to the
over-simplification, the reductionism, the exposure to facile
refutation, that are typical of many popular presentations. The
middle ground of laying it out simply and accurately, of saying
it as it actually is in forthright Anglo-Saxon, is rare, probably
because this presupposes deeper mastery of the thought than is
at the disposal of many interpreters of Bultmann. But Perrin has
it! For example (p. 46), Perrin's straightforward making-sense
of Bultmann's use of the term "eschatology," a use which for
most people must seem arbitrary, in that they are not able to
derive it from the common-sense meaning of the term: "The line
of reasoning here might be described somewhat as follows. Eschatology is the teaching concerning the way in which God will put
an end to the old world and establish a new. In the New Testament this is often expressed by such ideas as the coming of Jesus
on a cloud as Son of man to judge the world. But the point is
that God did not bring the world to an end in that way; he brought
it to an end by making authentic existence possible. So eschatology is teaching concerning the way in which God has made
authentic existence possible." What a straightforward English
Bultmann!

Bultmann is quite rightly analyzed as a basically consistent thinker, without major shifts in position once he had moved into dialectic theology. Where this generalization might be suspected has to do with the problematic position of Bultmann's book on Jesus, which seems to be preaching, within a theological system that does not consider the historical Jesus kerygmatic and explicitly in retrospect defines the book as not kerygmatic. Over against attempts to smooth out this ambiguity in favor of attributing greater importance to the historical Jesus in Bultmann's theology, Perrin (p. 58) has evened out this unevenness in what is I think clearly the direction indicated by the whole Bultmannian position, even if not made adequately clear in that ingenious book itself: "It is most important to stress here the two points that, in the first place, Jesus is in this respect no different from Plato, Goethe or Shakespeare, and that, in the second place, the challenge of the encounter with the words of Jesus to our self-understanding is not a challenge that can lead to the self-understanding of faith."

It is in the nature of the series that the book is not an Auseinandersetzung. Yet the careful systematic ordering of the whole, the highly selective concentration on crucial essays and passages, the ability to avoid clutter and lay bare the basic structures, the sensitive formulation that defies criticism by the most pedantic or fastidious--such traits betray the hand of one in full mastery of the material. E.g. the one instance where Perrin is explicitly critical he is also self-critical, i.e. he

analyzes the degree of relevance to be attached to the criticism
and does not lose sight of the valid point Bultmann is scoring
(pp. 78-81): Bultmann's "definition of myth is too broad and
clumsy. . . one of the few points at which I believe Bultmann
to be vulnerable to criticism . . . But if that is the case, then
it means that we have to go further in the direction toward which
Bultmann has pointed us--and he would be the first to cheer us
on our way! . . . One can raise questions about his understanding
of myth and still not have scratched the surface of his program."

It is with remarkable directness that a very balanced judgment on the whole of Bultmann's undertaking is presented on (pp.
87-89): "It is here that his greatness lies: in the way in which
he has succeeded in holding fast to the essentials of a deeply
theological tradition while accepting a radically secular view
of the world. It is my opinion that his critics have failed to
match him at this point: either they have abandoned some aspect
of the former or they have failed to come to grips with the latter
. . . This is what Bultmann is doing and it is hard to imagine a
way of doing it more relevant to the reality of man, the world
and the universe as we are being forced to recognize it today."

Perhaps the most impressive instance of Perrin's capacity to
lay hold of Bultmann's thought at its profoundest depths is in
his straightforward presentation (p. 29) of what Entschlossenheit,
"which may be translated 'resolve' or 'decision'," actually
means: "What happens in the moment of choice is that man chooses
resolutely to accept the certainty of death and the nothingness

of human existence. In doing this he achieves authentic existence because he now has no necessity to delude himself about his
being-in-the-world. We may say that he comes to know that it
is bounded by death and limited by the facts of life, and in the
resolve to accept this he finds the power to go through with it."

BIBLIOGRAPHY OF THE WORKS OF

NORMAN PERRIN

BOOKS

The Kingdom of God in the Teaching of Jesus. London:
SCM Press and Philadelphia: Westminster Press, 1963.

Rediscovering the Teaching of Jesus. London: SCM Press
and New York: Harper and Row, 1967.

The Promise of Bultmann. In the series, The Promise of
Theology, ed. Martin Marty. Philadelphia and New York:
J. B. Lippincott.

What is Redaction Criticism? In Guides to Biblical
Theology: New Testament Series, ed. Dan O. Via, Jr.
Philadelphia: Fortress Press, 1969.

ARTICLES

"The Kerygmatic Theology and the Question of the Historical Jesus," Religion in Life, 29 (1959-60), 86-97
[Written in conjunction with W. R. Farmer].

"New Testament Studies Today," Candler Advocate, 3
(1961), 2-3; 10-11.

"Faith, Fact and History," Christian Advocate (Dec. 20,
1962), 7-8.

"The Challenge of New Testament Theology Today," Criterion IV, 2 (Spring, 1965), 1-10.

"Mark XIV. 62: The End Product of a Christian Pesher
Tradition?" New Testament Studies, 12 (1965-66),
150-155.

"The Wredestrasse becomes the Hauptstrasse: Reflections
on the Reprinting of the Dodd Festschrift," Journal of
Religion, 46 (1966), 296-300.

"The Son of Man in Ancient Judaism and Primitive Christianity: a Suggestion," Biblical Research, 11 (1966)
17-28.

"New Beginnings in Christology," Journal of Religion,
46 (1966), 491-496. [Review article of R. H. Fuller,
The Foundations of New Testament Christology].

"The Parables of Jesus as Parables, as Metaphors, and
as Aesthetic Objects: A Review Article," Journal of
Religion, 47 (1967), 340-346.

ARTICLES, cont'd

"Recent Trends into the Christology of the New Testament,:
in Transitions in Biblical Scholarship, ed. J. C. Rylaarsdam. Essays in Divinity, VI (Chicago: University of
Chicago Press, 1968), 217-233.

"The Son of Man in the Synoptic Tradition," Biblical
Research, 13 (1968), 1-23.

"The Composition of Mark IX. 1," Novum Testamentum, 11
(1969), 67-70.

"The Creative Use of the Son of Man Traditions by Mark,"
Union Seminary Quarterly Review, 23 (1967-68), 237-265.

"The Challenge of New Testament Theology Today," in New
Testament Issues, ed. Richard Batey. Harper Forum
Books (New York: Harper and Row, 1970), pp. 15-34; also
published by SCM Press, London, 1970, pp. 15-34.
[=article in Criterion, IV, 2 (Spring, 1965).]

"The Literary Gattung 'Gospel' -- Some Observations,"
Expository Times, 82 (October, 1970), 4-7.

"The use of (para)didonai in Connection with the Passion
of Jesus," in Der Ruf Jesu und die Antwort der Gemeinde.
Festschrift f. J. Jeremias zum. 70 Geburtstag, ed.
E. Lohse (Göttingen: Vandenhoeck & Ruprecht, 1970),
204-212.

TRANSLATIONS

J. Jeremias, "The Qumran Texts and the New Testament,"
Expository Times, 70 (1958-59), 68-69.

J. Jeremias, "The Lord's Prayer in Modern Research,"
Expository Times, 71 (1959-60), 141-146.

J. Jeremias, The Sermon on the Mount. London: Athlone
Press, 1961.

J. Jeremias, The Question of the Historical Jesus.
Philadelphia: Fortress Press, 1964.

J. Jeremias, The Eucharistic Words of Jesus. London:
SCM Press and New York: Scribners, 1966.

BOOK REVIEWS

D. Bosch, Die Heidenmission in der Zukunftschau Jesu.
Journal of Biblical Literature, 79 (1960), 188-189.

E. Käsemann, Exegetische Versuche und Besinnungen I.
Journal of Biblical Literature, 80 (1961), 294-295.

K-P. Köppen, Die Auslegung der Versuchungsgeschichte
unter besonderer Berücksichtigung des Alten Kirche.

and M. Steiner, La Tentation de Jésus dans l'interpretation patristique de Saint Justin a Origène.

   Journal of Biblical Literature 81 (1962), 426-427.

W.A. Beardslee, Human Achievement and Divine Vocation
in the Message of Paul. Emory University Quarterly
18 (1962), 60-61.

James M. Robinson and John B. Cobb, eds. New Frontiers
in Theology I. The Later Heidegger and Theology.
Christian Advocate (Nov. 7, 1963), 19-20.

C.H. Dodd, Historical Tradition in the Fourth Gospel.
Journal of Religion, 44 (1964), 335.

"Against the Current," Review of G.E. Ladd, Jesus and
the Kingdom. Interpretation, 19 (1965), 228-231.

Bible Key Words from Kittel, Vol V. Christian Advocate
(Dec. 30, 1965), 18.

H. Anderson, Jesus and Christian Origins. Journal of
Religion, 48 (1965), 254-55.

"A Pertinent Distinction," Review of M. Kähler, The
So-Called Historical Jesus and the Historic Biblical
Christ, ed. and trans. by Carl E. Braaten. Christian
Century, 82 (Feb. 17, 1965), 214.

E. Käsemann, Exegetische Versuche und Besinnungen II.
Journal of Biblical Literature, 84 (1965), 62-63.

H.H. Rowley, The Relevance of Apocalyptic. 3rd ed. rev.

and D.S. Russell, The Method and Message of Jewish Apocalyptic.

   Journal of Religion, 45 (1965), 165-166.

W.D. Davies, The Setting of the Sermon on the Mount.
Journal of Religion, 45 (1965), 54.

BOOK REVIEWS, cont'd

W.G. Kümmel, Heilsgeschehen und Geschichte: Gesammelte
Aufsätze, 1933-1964. Journal of Religion, 46 (1966), 335.

E. Best, The Temptation and Passion. Society for New
Testament Studies, Monograph Series, II. Journal of
Religion, 46 (1966), 318-319.

Feine, Behm, Kümmel, Introduction to the New Testament.
Trans. by A.J. Mattil. Journal of Religion, 46 (1966),
506-507.

Daniel Fuller, Easter Faith and History. Harvey K.
McArthur, The Quest through the Centuries. J.F. Peter,
Finding the Historical Jesus. Journal of Religion,
46 (1966), 396-399.

"Wrestling with History," Review of The Bible in Modern
Scholarship. Papers Read at the 100th Anniversary of
the S.B.L., ed. Philip Hyatt. Christian Century, 83
(April 6, 1966), 433.

"Lukan New Wave," Review of Studies in Luke-Acts, ed.
Leander Keck and Louis Martyn. Christian Century, 83
(Sept. 7, 1966), 1081-82.

"The Quest Simplified," Review of J.F. Peter, Finding
the Historical Jesus. Christian Century, 83 (March 2,
1966), 273-274.

"Biblical Scholarship in a New Vein," Review of Dan O.
Via, Jr. The Parables: Their Literary and Existential
Dimension. Interpretation, 21 (1967), 465-469.

W.D. Davies, Invitation to the New Testament. Journal
of Religion, 47 (1967), 82.

"Putting Back the Clock," Review of Wolfhart Pannenberg,
Jesus--God and Man. Christian Century, 85 (Dec. 11, 1968),
1575-76.

"Theological Impasse," Review of Dietrich Ritschl, Memory
and Hope. Christian Century, 85 (April 10, 1968), 456-457.

O. Cullman, Salvation in History. Journal of Religion,
49 (1969).

Morna D. Hooker, The Son of Man in Mark. Journal of
American Academy of Religion, 37 (1969), 92-94.

J. Jeremias, The Prayers of Jesus. Journal of Religion,
49 (1969), 406-407.

BOOK REVIEWS, cont'd

> C.G. Montefiore, The Synoptic Gospels. Journal of Religion 50 (1970), 118-119.
>
> John Reumann, Jesus in the Church's Gospels: Modern Scholarship and the Earliest Sources. Encounter, 31 (Winter, 1970), p. 73.

IN PREPARATION

Books

> An Introduction to the New Testament for College Students, for Harcourt, Brace and World.
>
> The Gospel of Mark: A Commentary for the Hermeneia Series to be published by Fortress Press.

IN THE PRESS

Articles

> "The Christology of Mark: A Study in Methodology," Journal of Religion, 51 (July, 1971).
>
> "The Modern Interpretation of the Parables and the Problem of Hermeneutics," Interpretation, 25 (Spring, 1971).
>
> "Reflections on the Publication in English of Bousset's Kyrios Christos," Expository Times, 83 (1971-72).